SUNDAY MEDITATIONS for LIBERAL RELIGIOUS WORSHIP

SUNDAY

MEDITATIONS

FOR LIBERAL RELIGIOUS WORSHIP

By

PETER TUFTS RICHARDSON

Published by
RED BARN PUBLISHING
22 Mechanic St.
Rockland, ME 04841

www.redbarnrockland.com

ISBN-13: 978-0-974-1152-6-9

Photographs by Peter T. Richardson
Book Design by Peter and Eleanor Richardson
Cover Design and Printing by:
Custom Museum Publishing, Rockland, ME

To congregations

in

KENNEBUNK, MAINE

and

ANDOVER, MASSACHUSETTS

who first listened and responded to most of these meditations.

FOREWORD

With this collection of meditations I hope to add to the enrichment of liberal religious worship. They flow best of course when surrounded by silence and music which is at least a third of the worship experience. And worship points beyond itself to the imperatives of spiritual growth and work for social wellbeing, both generated and supported in congregational life.

An acquaintance with the content of these 65 poems and stories will quickly reveal my tendency to see our human experiment on this planet as a spiritual emergence. There are instances of exploring our mythic origins but also the present as it unfolds beyond itself. When our inheritance in all branches of human religious culture is appreciated we must find room to hold and absorb into our living an appreciation of shared human kinship. All insights, all wisdom, the presence of all spiritual heroes, saviors, sages, teachers and exemplars, all the gods/ goddesses, have a human face.

Most of all, these meditations are my own. They came through the experiences and internal fires of my own journey. They express my unique expression of what it is to be human. And thus I hope you will recognize in them our shared humanity.

Peter Tufts Richardson
January 2, 2009

INTRODUCTION

This collection of meditations is generally arranged with reference to the seasons. Some are quite specific and occasional and others are so general they may be used nearly any time of the year.

All photographs included are my camera work. I see the camera as an extension of ministry in a public that receives well over half its intake of information and inspiration through visual images.

Please do not interrupt the flow of worship with announcing credits for any of these meditations. If however they are reproduced in print or permanent recorded form, please give proper credit. If you have altered wording here or there simply add after the credit, "adapted."

You may find this collection of poems mainly grist for your own mill. There is no substitute for writing meditations from your own experience and insight. With weekly writing, remarkably, your work will improve. About the time you "retire" they may even be good. Then, of course, publish them for your colleagues. Meanwhile, I hope you will find what follows useful.

OUT OF THE VOID

Out of the void
comes life
thrilling the senses,
smell, touch, taste, sight, sound,
experiences
opening the brain,
spilling out meanings.
Out of the void
comes life.

Out of memory's void
come recollections of life's past
exciting old pathways
familiar to the mind's censors:
old fears and terrors,
old lusts and desires,
old nostalgias of place and experience
cascading through present moments,
back again into forgotten regions.
Memory's void
constitutes memory's life.

Out of the electronic void
are projected sights and sounds
for four hundred million eyes.
Out of black come flowing messages
hawking soap, beer, wheeled vehicles,
whirling through the brain
to be lost in a receeding fury of blackness again.
Out of the electronic void
come silly humor, violence,
dancing and singing, news bits,
all lost again in fade-to-black.
Out of the electronic void
comes electronic life.

Out of the void
comes the whirlwind of God,
spiritual things
in forest grove,
in temple sanctuary,
in seaside solitude,
in moments of illumination,
the presence present,
then fading to quietude
out into life again.
Out of the void
comes spiritual life.

Out of the void
come experiences
thrilling the senses
opening the brain.
Out of memory's void
come reflections of time lived.
Out of the electronic void
come imitations of experiences
for responsive witness of images.
Out of the whirlwind
of spiritual moments
comes buoyancy of soul.
Out of the void
comes life.

May we, in this moment
sense the void,
before us and after us,
sense the presence
whirling towards us,
towards this moment,
to be wrested from the void,
to be experienced, absorbed, lived, released
back again to rush into the darkness.
Know this time, find it, hold it, live it, lose it,
for out of the void comes, again, life,
life everlasting.
Out of the void
comes life.

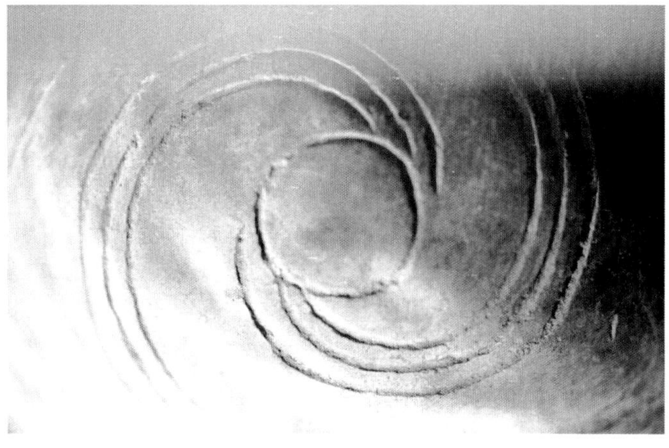

TREE: IT IS THERE

Form a picture of one tree
in your mind's eye,
not any tree but the tree you know intimately
in your life.
When you walk by, or drive by,
you know it is there.
It is there.

Just the thought of someone cutting
this one tree down
will send feelings of panic to your heart.
For this tree is not for lumber.
It is for patient growing,
past seven, past ten generations
to be there,
to companion hope.

Maple beside the street.
Oak standing in the field.
Pine beside the pond.
Apple tree on the hillside.
Magnolia beside the door.

Each day you greet this tree
for it is your essential connection
to earth and sky:
roots reaching inward to the center,
limbs reaching outward to moving air
and the stars.

Your tree is your assurance
for this day,
of graceful continuity,
rising to meet any eventuality
in storm or calm.

In its branches
life comes to rest,
winged life in need of support,
the restless to be restored,
the tired to be sheltered.

Beneath it in summer
we find shade from the sun,
a canopy against the rain;
and in winter we may look outward
along trunk and limbs
to the moving heavens beyond.

Tree standing between worlds
provokes contemplation to enlightenment,
shelters worship,
holds earth's sacrifice
for eternity.

Companion in the day
rising in the landscape,
consolation of life ongoing
through four seasons,
greening, growing, giving harvest
in generous colors,
standing in hope for returning life.

Familiar form for every day
unchanging in its essence,
standing steady in all turmoil,
transforming from its essence
responding to seasons of life.

It only asks that you pause
in your busyness,
pause to embrace this one fixed form
in a landscape of perpetual change,
while it yet stands for you.
For it is there for now.
It is always there.

SMELL OF SPRING

From hidden places welling,
a deep joy rising,
I smelled the soil
awaken.

Nine days early
before equinox,
earth prepares
spring.

Does it hurt
millions of micro organisms
should the ground
refreeze?

And peepers
climbing from swamps,
or salamanders under damp leaves
hatching?

I have no knowledge
of delicate thermostats
in tiny creatures
stirring.

Twigs of maple
swelling pink
draw the eye to gaze
upward.

A longer light
through brown membranes
kindles deep inside
a greening.

Birds chatter at dawn
in new crescendos of song,
an increased intensity
building.

A warm winter
offers up its last ice
in wind cooled nights
waning.

I have felt a disappointment
without the grip of cold,
fallen snow smothering frozen ground,
white.

It now seems late
when the smell of spring
awakens spiral stirrings
within.

The balance has tipped,
earth prepares her renewal,
green stirrings beneath brown
appearances.

With some regret
I too am shifting inexorably
to anticipations of renewal,
expectant.

I too grow towards spring,
feel a vague welling within,
origins of a joy emerging
to birth.

BLOSSOMS UPON THE BODY OF EARTH

Some time in the heavy morning air
a bird flew into my window
and broke its neck.

I found its perfect body
lying still on the step below,
little feet and gray feathers
with an iridescent green yellow sheen,
lovely symmetry and design,
beautiful, cold.

There is an awe and reverence
when we view the dead.
I could not move this body.
I could not intervene, not yet.

The day grew damp
and wind blew blossoms
from the weeping cherry
swirling down upon the ground,
down upon the body of the bird,
gently embracing pink petals
honoring the dead in the dusk.

In the morning, early,
darkness was broken
by the calling in of the dawn
in countless songs
of exultant joy.

Forgotten was this tragedy
moved to the side in the night.
As I picked it up
I noticed its belly
fleshy red, hollowed out.
It was time
to return this body to earth.

Goddess of Earth:
which gives birth
to lovely living forms.
God of Sky:
in which wings soar,
ascend, and fall.
Bodhisattva Avalokitesvara,
sound that illumines nature
Tara, Kwan Yin,
hearers of the weeping of the world:

May we attend the tiny dramas of earth unfolding,
winged birds and blossoms,
trees abundant.
May each flower
bring wonder,
every petal opening —
awe,
and in the wind swirling
of blossoms
upon the body of earth —
reverence
in the soul.

LIFE FORGETS

"Now there arose a new king over Egypt,
who did not know Joseph."

The world forgets its past.
Life forgets. Tragedies, great setbacks,
promises, dreams, joys, accomplishments:
we shall forget them all.

Memories, yes, they tarry awhile.
Vignettes of experience stay even for decades.
But the flesh and blood, the living presence,
it perishes quickly.

"Now there arose a new king over Egypt,
who did not know Joseph."

Do you really believe Egypt would remember
the dreams, the plans, the gathering into barns,
and the great feeding
when plague and hunger reigned?

No. Gratitude lasted a year or two.
Elders told the story, then died.
Vague references were entered by scribes
into annals commissioned by dead kings.

Storytellers and poets weave warnings, meanings.
Wandering minstrels sing for the heart.
But rising with each dawn, tending fields,
keeping ledgers, watching over children; we forget.

"Now there arose a new king over Egypt,
who did not know Joseph."

When your grandmother died
you could not control the tears.
The heart of the family emptied.
Her ever-present voice was stilled.

But now you rest in her chair
without a moment's thought of her.
Her voice may even speak to you
in a floating moment, faint, detached.

Life is always lived today.
Histories abstract make hollow alarms.
Vietnam is forgotten and the great holocausts,
volcanoes that covered the sun, famines.

Old ethnic grudges and atrocities
feed only new rages and flaws of character.
The deranged and demagogic have selective memories.
They distort the covenant of life.

"Now there arose a new king over Egypt,
who did not know Joseph."

Listen only to your human heart.
That is what your grandmother gave you long ago.
Listen to the bird song of this morning.
Place your feet only on the resilient ground.

The embrace of your lover is present to you,
the singing voices of playing children,
cool winds from the sea,
warm sun falling upon your shoulders.

"Now there arose a new king over Egypt,
who did not know Joseph."

Yes, these histories linger
and you will know in your bones
when there are Red Seas to cross.
For now, breathe deeply; step into today's gratitude.

ONE OF US WALKED IN GALILEE

One of us walked in Galilee
Two thousand years ago.
One of us spoke simply of flowers in the field,
of landlords and tenants,
of plowing fields, sowing seed, harvesting,
of brides and bridegrooms at weddings,
of honoring a Sabbath each week,
of feeding the hungry,
clothing the naked,
of the life of lepers, prostitutes, tax collectors, prisoners,
of lives that are to be honored
even if humble or mean.
He was comfortable with women or men equally,
he healed the blind, the lame, the paralyzed,
he resolved mental illness, chased away demons.
His touch was the touch of life.
One of us walked in Galilee
two thousand years ago
and he affirmed life.

When he was born angels sang
and the wise journeyed, paused, adored.
He was a gift of God.

Mary pondered this miracle in her heart.
Joseph reflected as he wielded saw and hammer on
wood.
Jesus conversed with temple elders at age twelve,
disappeared from sight for 15 or 18 years more,
struggled in the wilderness,
emerged to be baptized.

One of us walked in Galilee
two thousand years ago.
He spoke as one having authority.

He confounded scribes and Pharisees
    -- the Pharisee crossed to the other side
    but the Samaritan knelt down and helped
    the man who was hurt -
The rich young ruler could not adjust;
    it would be easier to drive a camel through the
    eye of a needle.
He left his father and mother.
    He let the dead bury their dead.
He gave Caesar's coin back to Caesar.
    He took note of the widow and her mite.
He drove money changers from the Temple
    and wept for Jerusalem and for Lazarus.
He celebrated the Passover with his friends,
    Gave his body and his blood for them.

One of us walked in Jerusalem
    two thousand years ago.
A gift of God,
    he was crucified on the Tree of Life.
From Jesse he was descended
    and they nailed him to a cross.
From Mary's womb he was born,
    of Divine and of earth.
From the tomb he rose again
    to walk for a time with disciples.
He ascended into clouds
    from earth back to sky
    to be with us always.

Fountains of water flow from Christ clouds
    through forests and fields of life.
And the judgments of life are there
    -- Christ of the large eyes and firm jaw
    to judge --
    what we have and have not done
        in compassion, for justice
    on this earth of joys and sorrows.

One of us walked in Galilee
    two thousand years ago.
We are born of the Tree of Life
    suffer its pain
    reach for joys of our ascent into the heavens.

One of us walked in Galilee
    heart to love,
    hands to heal,
    mind and spirit
        to attract earth
        into sky,
    to die and to be born in spring.

LIFE SACRIFICED, LIFE GAINED

Walking, trees stretching overhead,
I see great limbs extending bare to the east.
I know there is change
out there in every twig,
change I cannot see.

Lilac bushes wait for their season.
I know inside life flows.
Inside a drama is filling the world
I cannot see.

Just outside Argos I saw an olive tree
I shall never forget.
Two feet off the ground ran a scar full around
where it had been felled,
only to grow back to the very edge of its life,
reborn, a full tree again.
The impulse, memory, aspiration,
are not for me to know.

Under snow and mold
under old oak leaves flattened grey,
under brown blades of grass
lie green transformations.

Thorns warm along stems
thickly woven in my trellis.
Green leaves wait hidden
and roses bloom in some memory
waiting to be born.

Beneath patches of snow dripping in the sun
I cannot see yellow stems stretching.
White buds of crocus in the soil
will pierce through, purple.

Inside wood, a beetle,
inside soil, a grub curls round a dormant stem,
and mole waits for worm.
Hidden winter tunnels
soon will yield spring banquets
when the soil smells of life again.

My eyes itch and nose tingles
of pollen carried in the wind
flowing from blossoms far away
in another spring.

Song birds land in green yellowing willows.
Soon maples will turn red and orchards white.
Air will thicken with odors of lily and tulip
and wild rose.
A billion cells awaken in protest,
swelling misery, sorely itching,
will begin each morning in a sneeze.

Life many layered grows,
pushes forward and upward
to meet the sun.

Life sacrificed, life gained,
life engaging life,
whole universes hidden,
boiling in the soil,
pushing green into the light.

A cross, carved of living wood
is anchored into the ground.
Sacrificed is the tree
and the human body hung there.
In the rain, hewn wood
sprouts green shoots and leaves.
The tree of life is reborn
in the place of skulls.

To the sounds of howling dogs
and the laments of lingering mourners,
spring settles into exuberant torrents
of quickening green
and red, yellow, orange, white,
covering mud and trampled grass;
life rising in the thick air and thunder,
life that thrills heart
and stretches soul
into clouds of bright sunlight.

EASTER EGG ENCHANTMENT

Imagine, long ago,
a young child
looking for eggs
in deep grass.

Eggs blue, red, yellow
and green, hardest to find:
Striped eggs, others speckled,
a few fancy Lithuanian eggs.

Wandering through the grass
the child hoped to find one
before the older children
had them all.

It was exciting,
slogging through wet grass
in search
of speckled, striped, or plain eggs.

Why would a big rabbit
hop around
leaving colored eggs
in the grass?

There were shrieks of joy
as children found eggs.
Some had 5 or 6
but your basket still was empty.

You became desperate
as mothers pleaded with the others
to slow down
and give you a chance.

Then - there it was!
a yellow egg
with green speckles!
You grabbed it!

What joy.
What childish glee.
To see! To run!
To clutch in your tiny hand!

Now, be honest.
Can you remember
that excitement
from the inside?

Does it not seem
as if some other person,
not you,
entered such enchantment?

Can you really remember
the locomotion
of short, chubby
toddler legs?

Can you remember
the untied shoe
that tripped you up
and cracked the egg?

Can you remember
the ohs and ahs
when you held it up
to each and every significant adult?

Probably not.
It was too elemental
to remember,
too close to the ground.

That primitive life
was not you,
only the memory
of remembering remains.

So when the children you know
run and stumble around
in search of eggs,
don't even try remembering.

Just watch the happy children.
Loudly oh and ah
at cracked and dented eggs
in little hands.

And praise the hare
that hopped all around
in green grasses
laying eggs for Easter.

CROCUS BLOSSOMS

It was a warm October Sunday morning in 1966
when Catherine Hannum and thirty children
knelt together on the south lawn grass.

In some deep place Cathy knew
this would be her last October;
and perhaps the children knew too
from the special tenderness of her touch;
each child with a serving spoon,
and cardboard strip with a line drawn across
at the perfect depth for crocus bulbs.

They knelt together for an animated hour,
setting in the bulbs just so,
covering carefully, caring for the sod placed back,
tamping the ground.

It was a reverence, a trusting,
an acting upon faith that beneath
the grass fading in the fall sunlight,
beneath the coming snows of winter,
nestled securely in earth's soil,
the womb of life awaited spring.

In March Cathy died.
We spoke of her faithfulness
of many years in congregation.
We told stories of her annual cooking
of Election Day Dinners.
We spoke of her vocation,
"the flower lady of Kent, Ohio."
And we placed her body in the tomb
of her beloved earth.

Easter Sunday came in warm,
sun bright across the south lawn.
We gathered in quiet joy
crossing among a hundred crocus blossoms,
golden yellow and purple in the greening grass.
There was a special excitement among the children
and tears in the singing:
"Lo, the earth awakes again, Alleluia . . .
How our hearts leap with the spring!"

SPRING BODHISATTVAS

In singing of robins
at early dawn,

In the brightening skies
the yellow radiations of sun,

In the mists that gather
on the blades of grass,

In the scampering
of gray squirrels,

A thousand bodhisattvas
rise up out of the ground
in one mirage of sound.

In the soft pink
of the weeping cherry,

In the saturated yellow
of daffodils,

In the flaming red
of maples,

In the white filigree
of blossoming cherry,

A thousand bodhisattvas
rise up out of the ground
in one mirage of color.

Beneath the sound of locomotive
at the crossing,

Beneath the jet plane
roaring into landing,

Beneath the sound of car engine
delivering the Sunday paper,

Beneath the sound of sirens
of a far off emergency,

Spring comes forth
inexorably in the ground.

At work and career there is struggle
to keep our lives intact,

At home there is struggle
of wellbeing, fairness, nurture of all,

In towns there is struggle
to serve and not exploit,

In buying and selling there is struggle
to provide for, not to smother, life,

Bodhisattvas rise out of earth,
eternal, constant, compassionate,
To remind life that struggles
to see when earth opens into spring
that life may open too.

WINGS INDIGO IN THE DAWN

Picture yourself walking,
        ascending to the temple of your life.
You enter a forest of tall trees
        and hear softly their quiet presence.
As you continue on the path
        you awaken to rushing water beside you
        in the cascading mountain stream.
The ground beneath your feet
        is dusty and rocky.
        You step around large stones.
        You touch ledges and boulders beside the path.
You feel your leg muscles tighten
        as you climb.
The path bends around a large cedar
        where people rest sitting on gnarled roots.
The sun that warmed your back
        when the journey began
        now filters gray through drifting mist
        as the mountain intrudes a solitude
        in your pilgrim climb.
You enter the One Pillar Gate,
        auspicious,
        as the journey begins in new earnestness.
The valley below gives up its sounds,
        muffled,

sounds of the world at work,
accustomed habits of dawn to dusk.
But now it is careful feet meeting
the unforgiving earth,
deeper breathing to sustain the journey.
Each step becomes attentive
more reflective
into the mountain.
Your foot scuffs loose a rock, rolling,
and you pick it up to hold, friendly and snug,
in your hand
as you enter the Gate of the Guardians
keeping safe the shadows
of mountain ravine
and hidden darkness in the trees.
Now the quiet sings
with the soft breezes in tree limbs.
enchanted with growing presence
of sheltering mountain surrounding.
Beside the path you find a large pile of rocks
stacks of smaller stones placed on larger
by pilgrim hands,
a pagoda of the spirit,
and the rock so comfortable in your hand
finds its place at the peak.
Sun filters through an open place in the trees
to illumine just the tiny peak
and a dragonfly lands
to dry its wings, iridescent in the light,
purple, red, green, indigo.
And you enter the Gate of Enlightenment,
floating in the sound of temple bells
beside the blue cloud of incense.
In blue cloud temple
you enter Hera's cave
below Buddha's golden Sumeru,
listen in Confucius' Apricot Grove,
feel the chiseled marks on Moses' stone,
see the red and yellow lilies of Christ's field,
embrace Mohammed's arching sky
and apprehend Lao Tzu's valley spirit
rising to assure you
of your return transformed.

For your life awaits you beyond the gates,
to engage trials and struggles
of living which sustains this journey.
And you will reenter to engage this life
with the wings of a dragon fly
and the residue of incense
filtering indigo in the gentle dawn
of each new day.

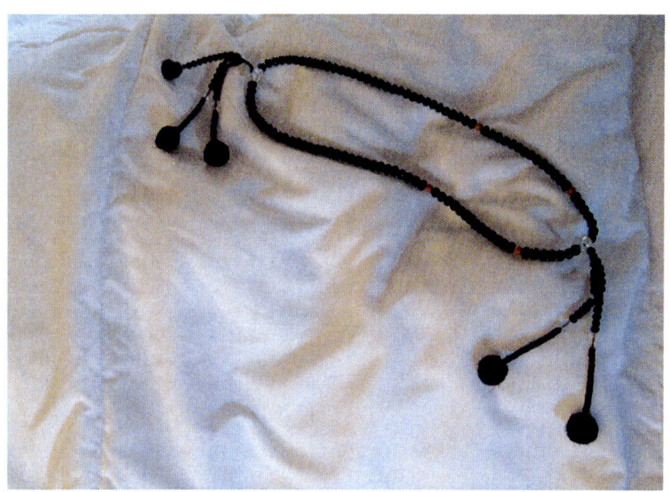

108 BEADS

Rub 108 beads in the hands
and a thousand prayers
          ascend, descend,
in the body of the world.

Walk on shells beside the sea
and a thousand crumble
          into sand
with every step, every wave.

Drive on snow
and a thousand flakes per second
          transform to water,
flowing, freezing, towards the river.

Fill the bird feeder
and a thousand thistle seeds
          are absorbed into flesh,
flying in currents of wind.

Combine oil with fire
and a thousand flames roar
          through furnaces
warming human homes.

Catch an idea with the mind
and a thousand others spin variations
into labs, homes, libraries, memories,
infinitely expanding collective understanding.

Rub 108 beads in the hands
and a thousand prayers
ascend, descend,
in the body of the world.

1000 prayers, 1000 grains of sand,
1000 flakes of water,
1000 seeds into winging,
1000 flames burning,
1000 variations of an idea.

Every motion, every moment,
is transforming.
Every wave dissolves
into the next wave.
Life to non life to life again,
animate with inanimate.

A thousand becomes one,
one becomes two,
two becomes four,
500 becomes a thousand,
a thousand becomes one.

Can the human form resist
transformations?
Can an idea or a feeling
endure beyond a moment?
Or a monument
beyond 5 thousand years?

Rub 108 beads in the hands
and a thousand prayers
ascend, descend,
in the body of the world.

BELTANE COMING

I once saw young ballerinas
dressed in delicate pastel dresses
dancing lightly around a May pole
on the lawn of Westminster Abbey.

I wondered if they had any idea
of what they were enacting!
Weaving green, gold, red, blue streamers,
stepping perfectly, precisely,
around the erect pole.

In ancient times we know
it was the ritual of fertility,
back before the advent of indoor plumbing
and daily showers,
back when clothing was coarse woven,
thick, worn for days.

The innocent ballerinas
imitating an ancient rite,
what could they know of frenzy?
of sweaty bodies leaping ecstatically,
of the weave coming closer to the pole
until they must slide by and over
each other like drunken seals in the surf.

We now enter a season
when the world explodes
with intoxicating energy
pushing out rebirth from within.

It is a sticky business pollinating
through blinding beauty
of red, pink, gold, green,
pulsating it all out there to be
smelled, tasted, consumed.

Would dainty ballerinas know
when the heat comes
an excitement rises
through every bird and beast,
wild expression
of earthen energy to express?

TAPESTRY OF LIFE

To find deep red leaves
        of the Japanese maple
unfolding before a field of pale green
        sugar maples!
To watch pink magnolia buds
        expand and burst into bloom!
To consider Judas tree purple
        beside green-green hemlock boughs!
To marvel at white blossoms
        appearing among tender young apple leaves!

I see them now and forever
        will dwell with them
in the tapestry of life,
        weaving red and yellow, green and blue.

Late afternoon sun illumines
        cat o nine tails
against the great salt marsh
        stretching fertile brown beyond!
Through the tangled gray
        lower limbs of pine
a red fox scampers effortlessly
        into the shadowed reaches of forest.
while geese rise from brackish waters
        filling the quiet with alarm.

I see them now and forever
        will dwell with them
in the tapestry of life,
        weaving red and yellow, green and blue.

One gray squirrel chases another
        round and round
upward into the arching oak limbs
        silhouetted in the western light.
Through reddened limbs of maple
        two brown does stand alert
hidden silhouettes against the whitened sky
        touched with purpled pink.

I see them now and forever
        will dwell with them
in the tapestry of life,
        weaving red and yellow, green and blue.

The dance has begun
        of heightened sensibility,
Beltane:
        imparting life to life.

A VOICE DIVINE

It is a glorious world we must leave,
at least for now;
Back to reality, if that is what we mean,
at least for now.

I remember when warm May breezes
brought to me the pungent smell of lilacs
so heavy my eyelids half closed.
I remember the gull's plaintive call
circling around far away
mixed in the sweetness.
And I could hear a car along South Main Street
tree by tree fading into its journey.
A motor boat in the harbor sputtering and droning
rounded the point and went away.
A bug hit the porch post
altered course, dazed, and disappeared.
Sun on the barn's south side
caused wood to snap in its warmth.
Oh, the feel of a gentle breeze falling across your face
mesmerized by an omnipresent scent
of lilac pollen.
Even the rocking chair stopped its rocking
as the mind entered its eternity.

It is a glorious world we must leave
          if that is what we mean.
Back to reality, at least for now,
          that has not left us now nor then.

A calling stirs us;
          the rocking chair moves again.
A voice Divine rouses us out of eternity
          to live, to bend this present time
          to move new melodies into being.
A voice Divine comes urgent
          through the peacefulness.
Driving purple lilacs back into their season
          it stirs old memories to new meaning.

It is a glorious world
          we must be leaving.
If that indeed is what we mean,
          memories, building upon memories,
          upon memories;
          we build melodies for a new world.

FATAL CRISIS

Arriving at 8 a.m. with paper and book
tea bags and a letter for my wife,
in a brown paper bag,
I peeked around the door into her hospital room.

She was not sitting up.
There was no smile;
only tubes,
labored breathing,
comatose.

"Better call Dr. Lashey."
He named the tumor.
"She will probably die before noon."

Later
after my step-daughter joined me,
after a friend on the staff
checked in, and tuned in,
we followed the bed
down an elevator
through a subterranean corridor,
bricks painted white,
steam pipes and sewer pipes

painted white,
white everywhere,
up another elevator
to the cat scan room.
We looked at before and after pictures
which showed what we knew
and we were amazed.

She died before noon
on her daughter's birthday.
We said good bye - together and alone -
several times
with her peaceful body, there.

The tears had come
and five ministers were there
and two from the church.
It was a convulsed and strangely lucid time.
We donated her kidneys and eyes
and whatever else could live.
The surgeons received our permission
to go in and see what had happened.

Her night nurse had stayed
and found me,
touched my arm and shoulder,
said, "I'm so sorry,"
and handed me the brown bag
with book and tea bags and letter.

FOR MOLLY

A feather falling upon water
is carried flowing, swirling,
peacefully to the sea,
rising and falling in the planetary tides.

Lost over the horizon,
ever rolling among the seven continents
        of our living,
traces are reflected brilliant
in the silver glow of evening.

These same nurturing energies
        ascend and descend
in the tree of life,
ascending through the ten limbs
to become a golden flower
that blooms but a day, a glorious day!

And then is carried in the wind,
swirling in the sun,
to replenish the earth
in new seeds of life.

How profoundly sad to feel such beauty
taken from firm branches.
Pervasive sadness wells within us
when earth takes back her own.

How glorious was the bloom,
how gentle but firm was the wind
that gathered that beauty in its embrace
and carried her to deepest memory.

We will listen acutely for awhile
to the sounds of the wind and the tides of the sea
to hear even one echo of her voice
        in the landscape
of all who listen in the silver light.

The heavy heart requires for its solace
the sorrow of sadness,
the catch in the flow of air to the lungs,
until dances in the drumbeat and fire
can evolve new pranic rhythms
for the atmosphere of each new day.

It is too early to know the unfolding pathway ahead.
Now we know only a great loss, a disruption,
a passage into the unknown,
confident only of a great love
and spiritual connection.

Glean wisdom from the many precious moments
of thirty years or thirty minutes with Molly.
Gather meanings in the reflections
of wind and water,
waving leaves and flowers,
familiar voices, places, images,
until they rise as a song in your heart,
a song bringing sadness and joy together
for new affirmations.

We know now as surely as we will ever know
how brief is our sojourn
in the companionship of life.
We move closer to our loved ones
in gentle kindnesses, in embrace of mutual affirmation.
We breathe deeply in gratitude for the gift of life,
and the blessing of Molly's life resonant in our hearts.

EVE/MY MOTHER'S WORK

for MOTHERS' DAY

I am her creation.
Conceived, gestated, floating in her womb,
she fed me, grew me,
threw me into the world,
held me and comforted me
from bright lights and sounds.
From Eve I was her creation.

She was huge, source of milk,
source of all needs.
I attuned to every nuance
of her munificence,
huge presence from Eve.

My older brother died at four months.
But this child was not destined to die early.
Eighteen years later my Mother learned why Elford Jr.
had died,
when my younger brother was diagnosed
with cystic fibrosis.
My brother, David, died eventually at age 36.
Her grief continued sixty-three years.

All three of us presented a challenge to raise.
I was a stubborn child; there was a war of wills;
I was her intellectual challenge.
My sister, Ann, was sensitive, thoughtful.
Her tantrums were rare but terrible;
my Mother's emotional challenge.
My younger brother lived, thin with a cough
but indomitable and fun;
her physical challenge.

When I was nearly four she was pregnant.
It was summer and hot.
I was sent to be with my great aunt for four months
when my brother was born.
My aunt was very different,
loving and doting, a second mother,
and the salt air and the sea rolled through my
consciousness,
as Mare, the great Mother from before Eve.

But we were my Mother's work, from Eve.
It was a stimulating time: views,
questions, interest, opinions, judgments, exploration.
It was a learning time, of imagination, of family,
siblings, father, chores, journeys;
of an omnipresent Mother person.

From Eve, a million years, Mother continuous,
has life been created, life like me.
My sister continued from my Mother
and her daughter now continues from Eve.
My daughters, too, continue from their Mother,
and they have five sons and a daughter.

Leaving Mother's home was gradual.
My father's presence understood what sons do.
Eventually he approved my vocation.
The vast Mother presence we love we must leave
to seek in the world a passage
only we can discover and create,
something new and ours.

But today is our Mothers' Day,
that great loving presence in our lives from Eve.
I have my journey, and my sister, hers,
and my brothers who died.
My Mother lives and my father in cherished memory.
My Mother lives from all time
of infancy, childhood, youth and my leavetaking
and the continual reunions of our lives.
My Mother lives in me and continues through my world,
from Eve she lives, she loves us since before time
and tomorrow she continues to be borne
in new worlds of life.

INGRAHAM
DIED
23, 1848,

FOR MEMORIAL DAY

The last one in my family
to serve on a battlefield
was Tilden Thomas II,
my great great grandfather.
His right hand was blown off
in the Civil War.

They lived in a small cape
on Warren Street.
I inherited a sugar and cream set
that belonged to his wife, Melinda Herrick.
She was a quiet person
with a kindly face.

A picture of Tilden shows him on a sidewalk
in his boiled white shirt
speaking with workers.

My family was fiercely abolitionist,
propelled in the freedom of Maine Baptist preaching.
No one ever thought to mention,
perhaps they did not know,
how Tilden Thomas felt about his life
in the long years after the war.
His picture was in the paper,
a veteran with his army hat.
My great aunt had his sword
by the window in the attic,
hanging over a ladder back chair.
I don't know what became of it.

There are, of course, many ways
to live through tragedy:
childbirth, tuberculosis,
wear and tear building stone walls,
falling from haylofts,
drowning from ships.
And yet all sort into place
among the generations.

We try to keep them all in memory,
the dour as well as the loving,
the high achievers along with plain simple folk.
They all have kept their appointment with life
that we too might live.

On this weekend we visit gravesites.
We trace across the faces of stones
for names and dates and cryptic sayings.
We place flowers and flags
in the ground.

Some will remain untended,
the abusers, the forgotten, the last of their lines.
Remember them too
in your compassionate heart.
Remember the soldier, the seamstress,
the mothers and maiden aunts,
the children who died so tiny,
the elders who told their stories
of the faithful dead, to the grateful living.

KNOXVILLE

We learned pure aggressive rage
fighting lions;
then returning to the arms of love,
aggression receding into a sea
of comfort, consolation.

What could be more potent
than to sacrifice oneself for one's companions?
-- a close cousin to revenge.
What could be more potent
than to sacrifice oneself to avenge
a wrong done to one's tribe?

Samson brooding in captivity,
when his seven locks of hair grew back,
avenged his defeat by Philistines
pulling down the pillars of the house
upon his enemies and himself
(the world's original suicide bomber).
His tribesmen and women
wrote poems of his valor, his sacrifice,
buried him with honor in the family tomb.

Last month, a man out of the blue
seated himself in the congregation
of the Knoxville, TN, U. U. Congregation.
He had been there before with his then wife.
Both had wandered away years before,
had divorced and were lost to view,
to any connection,
so far as anyone knew.

After years of lonely brooding
and unemployed, society's discard,
he reappeared and seated himself.
There was no joyful reunion
for nobody remembered.

The congregation had now become the focus
of long brooding projections by this stranger.
Its liberal outreach was now the cause of his woes.
It supported oppressed minorities, especially the gays.
It supported the liberation of women,
while he, unemployed, cast aside, anonymous,
drifted depressed in the shadows.
His one competence remained a gun.
His resentment, his blaming, his raging moods
pulsing, consuming, he set out
to kill the lion.

He seated himself towards the front
while hormones and readied genes
coursed through amygdala, hypothalamus,
no counter chemicals breaking a rising revenge.
Not even children singing could calm
the roiling Samsonian storm.
He began firing!
A large man rose and hurled himself
into this rage, pushing him to the floor,
dying there as others now held down

the intruder from dark atavistic violence
until police carried him away.
He will be punished.
He will not return to loving arms
of solace, of comfort.

"Greater love has no man than this,
that he lay down his life for his friends."
Consider the usher, Greg McKendry,
who rose in an instant
and hurled himself into gun and assailant.
In an instant the same chemical wash
coursed through amygdala, hypothalamus,
unchecked by doubts,
or considerations of self-preservation
-- he could have been one of us.
Now mourned by loving hands,
grateful hearts in grief,
traumatized friends
returning to each other,
comforting, consoling,
healing torn hearts
in a world needing justice.
Have compassion for the broken among us;
compassion for the loving who must prevail!

GRIEF TO GRATITUDE

Grief weighing in the heart brings you
to walk from garden path, to field, to forest,
to feel wind waving leaves overhead
in an otherwise still and deepening silence;
and you must slow to a mindful witness.

You can wonder that the trees are there,
rippling rows of bark,
arching limbs ascending,
twigs gaunt before the green mantle,
whispering, sending shadows shivering,
opening windows of momentary luminous light.

Walking in this darkening
restless standing presence
one question floats through the mind,
"Does the forest know I am here?"
Nothing comes back,
no message breaks through.

The path ends abruptly
in pond rocks and dry oak leaves
against still waters of a secluded pond.
You see sticks in the water and black leaves
swirled into fish nests.
Beyond is only still blackness
with a gray sheen of clouded sky
reflecting forest limbs and leaves.

You sit on a rounded stone,
lean back against roots
and stare at that placid darkness.
You can see no face
smiling out of the depths
of sky or waters.
You find no answer from the depths.
In your breathing there is a catch
of momentary grief and then quiet motion
as a sleepy sheen
clouds your sight
enchants the ear momentarily.

You awaken when rain drops reach your nose,
your arm, your neck.
It is a general rain.
The ground begins to offer up
an odor of humus.

Prickly sounds issue from a placid pond.
While the trees remain silent
lichens stretch outward.

It is time to leave wet rocks
for shelter under the canopy
of dripping leaves and heavy drops.
You keep walking,
abandon all thoughts of dryness
knowing field and garden path lie before you.

In your questions of forest and pond
sky has given you rain.
Pond has offered up sound of raindrops.
Forest has offered down sound of dripping leaves.
Soil has offered odors of dampness.
And all you could give is gratitude
in your surrender to the rain.

Surrender to the rain is all you can do,
surrender entirely, to each drop,
to dampness and dripping wetness.
From garden path, to forest, to pond,
to forest, field and garden path again
there is only surrender,
surrender to the great sky,
surrender to the waters,
abandoning all pretense, all privilege,
surrendering all grief to gratitude,
all questions to a path through the forest
and when grief flows into gratitude,
to be washed clean in rain.

FOURTH OF JULY

This red, white and blue
        on cloth,
remade colors
        from the old Union Jack,
has flown in various forms
        on battle fields
        and in military installations
        around the world.

Men have died under it,
        come home wrapped in it;
or alive, wrapped themselves in it
        and been elected
        to political office.

Women have sewn it together
and watched their sons and husbands
disappear over the horizon
and from life
following this piece of cloth.

So powerful is its allure
it is flown
or burned
whenever a speaker wants to be heard.
It rivets attention.

Our National Anthem
records a battle
and asks, “by dawns early light,”
if the flag is “still there.”

The red, white and blue cloth
is even brought into churches
(alongside flags for state and United Nations)
to rest motionless for contemplation.

But the church is also a place
where we separate symbols
from realities
where we elevate guides
to reveal larger truths
so that the symbols fall away
idolatries become expunged
and realities come in.

Flags will wave proudly
this Fourth of July
To remind us of the accomplishments
of our nation
among the scores of nations
of our earth.
Fireworks will honor it
in brilliant exuberance.

But remember also it is only a piece of cloth
that fades and stains and rots
in the fires of nature’s entropy.

Praise it for its witnessing.
Praise the principles
for which it stands.
But return home to live
in the realities, the spiritual realities,
which stand behind it,
and let the piece of cloth
have its day.

REMEMBERED IN THE FABRIC ONGOING

64

The wake of a ship waves and ripples for awhile,
a new pattern upon the waters.
Then by degrees the wake dissolves
into the ongoing energies at the interface
of water and sky.

So too each of us in our passage through life
throws out waves across the continuities
of community and landscape.
In due time we depart
and the waves of our passage subside
and are absorbed in life ongoing.

When a member leaves our midst,
an interest, an influence, a presence,
whatever was unique
is remembered in the fabric ongoing.
The disturbing, still disturbs.
The comforting, still comforts,
until eventually its source becomes indistinguishable
in the living of our lives.

History is filled with attempts
to push back the frontiers of memory,
to have our names endure beyond a generation or two.
Rameses III built colossal statues of himself.
Mohammed ascended to heaven in Jerusalem.
Melville wrote Moby Dick.
Only a few are remembered for a long time.
But how much can we remember
even of those we can name?
The human best is lost to any name,
is absorbed in the living,
enters the tides of time.

Today we vow to always remember each other!
And we shall cherish our memories!
But the best of all we have shared
has already entered our lives
and dissolved in our hearts.
We, even now, live our memories.
Beyond our farewells,
beyond the sound of our voices
and the touch of our hands,
and even our love for each other,
is the quality of our lives lived forward,

and our children's lives,
the living world,
long after our names are forgotten!

The wake of a ship waves and ripples for awhile,
a new pattern upon the waters.
Then by degrees the wake dissolves
into the ongoing energies at the interface
of water and sky.

TAKE A CHILD'S HAND

Summer is a time
        for noontime reflections
        under a sweltering sun,
and a time for evening walking
        under a clear sky
        with a billion stars.

Take a child's hand in your hand
        and walk.
Walk without speaking
        to listen and look.

Walk through forest
        with its shadows and poignant silence.
Walk past gnarled trees, boulders, bushes,
        on a carpet of leaves
        past flowers and rotten logs.

Walk into the field
        smelling grasses.
Pluck hot blueberries from low bushes.
        Find the tiny wild strawberry.
        Stare at ants busy about their hill.

Take a child's hand in your hand
        and walk.
Walk without speaking
        to listen and look.

Walk barefoot on hot sand
        along the high tide mark.
Take in the stench of dead seaweed
        watching fleas, flies
        and wizened gulls scavenge.
Leave tracks in the cool wet sand
        of the retreating tide
        and feel barnacles with the smoothness
        of steaming ledges in the sun.

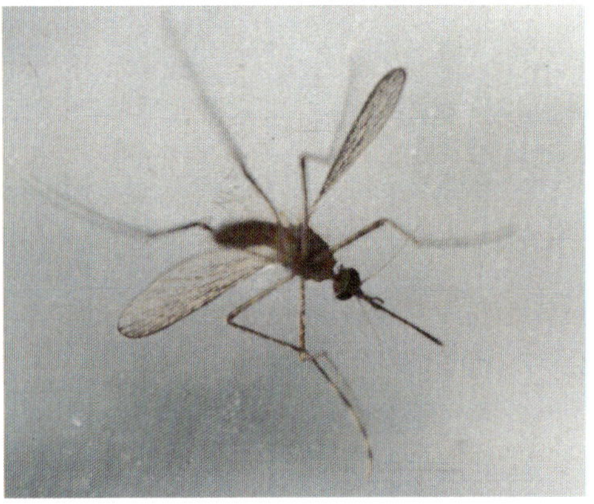

Take a child's hand in your hand
and walk.
Walk without speaking
to listen and look.

In the evening chase fireflies
in the long grass
and listen to crickets.
Sense the presence of swamp peepers
and glugging frogs.
You may hear an owl hoot
or bear calls from the hills.

Find a large lichen-covered ledge
and sit under the stars.
Lie back in the softness of the night
and watch for shooting stars.
Wonder at the mottled surface
of the moon, bright,
or obscured by a passing cloud.

Take a child's hand in your hand
and walk.
Walk without speaking
to listen and look.

SUMMER STORM

Summer sounds warm and dry
from cicadas high in trees
dry limb upon dry limb
for a lethargic evening,
carrion crows watching
high in an elm.

Horizon sounds of thunder rolling
in roiling clouds coming;
Soon we hunker down
in expectation.

Lightning strikes, searing streaming
through helpless trees,
wounding, numbing terror.

Thunder silences all sounds,
enfolds, absorbs, destroys.
It will take a powerful dance
to bring us back.
We once lived in trees –
high nests gently swaying,
now burning.

The rain descends
dripping from scalp and nose and chin
falling from shoulders, hips, knees.

soaking into ground,
washing leaves and blades of grass,
the soft odor of roots swelling.

Moon is revealed
in glimpses among rushing clouds.
We breathe clear air
in the survivors' peace.

First light brings song.
A glistening flora unfolds and fauna stirs
opening melodies, turning eastward;
sounds of human awakening –
engines, doors opening,
coffee bubbling,
church bells tolling
across centuries.

Stretching, walking, bipedal running
across millennia –
inhaling exhaling.
In this moment
life begins again.

SCRIPTURES

"God is love" proclaims the *First Epistle of John;*
and in *Leviticus:*
"If a man lies with a male as with a woman, both of
them have committed an abomination;
they shall be put to death."

"God is love."

There are myriad verses of scripture in the world.
Our human culture is deep.
There are hundreds of thousands of rhymes and reasons
  to discover, to take to heart, to live by.

For those who would love,
  they will find love.
For those who would hate,
  they will find hate.

"There is nothing new under the sun," said Koheleth.

To discover the truth of scriptures;
  look into the eyes of the reader of verses.
  Do you see hate there, or love?

To discover the humanity of scriptures;
examine the intentions of the reader.
Look into their heart.
Is there a warmth there?
Is there an embrace?
Is there compassion there?
Is there generosity?

To discover the strength of scriptures;
search for the soul of the reader.
Is there a foreboding judgment there,
harsh and barren emanations?
Or are there radiations of love
which affirm, support, sustain?

"God is love."
There should be no stoning to death
of those who embrace.

Scripture is as true, as humane, as strong for us
as the depth of heart and soul is for us.

There are a million verses there for us
from six continents.

There is beauty there
to inspire love in our hearts.

There is also fear and terror there
to inflame those who have lost generosity
of heart.

Scripture gives us the rattle of death
and the embrace of love.

Every child has this inheritance
to fuel the emptiness
or to open the fullness.

May they find among us gathered
the community of love.

May they find opened here
pages which proclaim:

"God is love."

ALLAH

At Saquara I encountered the desert
North of Imhotep's Step Pyramid.
To my right: 1000 miles of sand;
To my left: hidden behind dunes, the Nile.
Facing south: the sun broke over the pyramid's peak
pouring white light on all slopes
        like molten lead.
The heat was heavy,
Illumination rooted my feet upon the shifting ground.
Embracing all was the omnipresent sky.

I stood in the presence of vast forces
        ever shifting eternal presence,
a sojourner who could only respond
with humility in my smallness,
with elation in my participation:
        to breathe of this expanse,
        to smell this dryness,
        to taste the dust of ages,
        to touch grains of impermanence,
        to hear stirrings of eternal wind.

Here I learned of limitless horizons
        beyond my knowing.
Here I learned of impermanence
        the wearing away, the shifting,
        the fading of my footprints.
Here I understood the utter indifference
        of sky and sun, of earth
        and the dimming morning moon.
My life held no more permanence
        than a mote of churning dust beneath my shoes.

Eleanor reappeared from behind a mound
that long ago had been a tomb.
We walked to rejoin Mohammed Abd El Daime,
our driver.
Moving back across barren sands
into the valley of rice and vegetables,
water buffaloes in canals,
to rejoin mother Nile.

That evening, hearing the call to prayer
penetrate my consciousness
from a thousand Cairo minarets,
I could only think of fathomless sky,
endless shifting ground,
flowing light upon rock,
and the hot dry wind
gathering dreams and visions,
hopes and despairs alike,
into an eternal embrace.
Allah, The Compassionate, The Merciful,
The Only One.

Hearing the call to prayer at the doorway
of Al-Rafai Mosque,
Entering into noon prayer at Al Azhar Mosque
with one hundred men,
Hearing the call reverberate from a mosque above
while I meditated in the ruins
of Luxor Temple.
I could only think of vast sky
and shifting dust,
breathing deeply of dry air, filling my inmost parts,
life giving, life taking.

You cannot bargain with uncompromising desert.
It is what it is.
You can only surrender.
Breathe deeply. Wonder. Accept.
In the mosque you wash dust
from your body.
You walk barefoot upon the carpet.
You surrender:
as the longing for life
and life abundant
ascends in haunting clarity
through a vast emptiness
to the Eternal.
Allah, The Compassionate, The Merciful,
The Only One.

TAKE YOUR TROUBLES TO THE NILE

Even in the heart of the city
desert dust floats gently in
and settles on every leaf and roof
reminding us of its pervasive presence.

"Take your troubles to the Nile"
is the one counterbalance
to the great dryness,
the powerful Nile sweeping to the sea
the silt of ages.

The desert sky,
the flowing Nile,
Father Sun,
Mother River.

The mosque sits square
minarets pointing skyward
courtyard open
Qiblah pointing eastward
over sands, to Mecca.

While the river flows and floods
fields prosper
wheat, oranges, cauliflower,
bring happy prosperity.
The land and life are good.

And when times are sparse or sad
the people come, alone, together, in the dusk
to sit beside the waters of the Nile,
to seek solace and reconciliation,
to feel the healing presence
flowing eternal to the sea.

Dawn breaks
the red sun rises through a brown blue dusty haze
until it ascends clear and hot
omnipresent, all seeing, all consuming,
illumining all distinctions,
possessing all diversities
in one kingly unity.

There is no escape
from the omnipotent beam
no hiddenness
before such penetration.

At apex only footprints
disappearing - reappearing
ever receding over horizons vast.

Limitless openness
brings you to your knees in submission,
in supplications for justice and mercy,
the very gifts the desert withholds
but the clear, remote God gives.

Allah, the merciful
the mighty protector
the compeller, subduer.
bestower, provider,
all knowing, exalter
the great ONE (Ya - ‘Azim).

Afternoon light slants from the West
trees, sand, sky warmly glow.
Dusk rises from the valley
a restless world hurries home
while at the center, flowing, silent,
earth reclaims all her hidden diversity
and people come to sit
quietly listening to the waters
of comfort, solace, healing --
“Take your troubles to the Nile”:
wait, patient and calm, in the dark.

For SARVA DHARMA SAMELANA

Bangalore, India, 1993

To the red sun we bow.
To our whirling blue and white planet
we call out gratitude in our hearts for our home.
To the surrounding green trees
we listen for the call of birds, the song of life.
We open our beings to all sound,
from east and west, north and south,
OM sound, to lift us in its vibrations,
to center us here with our friends.
May eternal music flow through us
on resonating strings of our humanity.

We encircle the globe in recognition of our kinfolk,
in the diversity of one human family,
the dance of life in many branches
of our human culture.
May we give praise that our spirituality is not the same
as that of our neighbors,
that we can learn and grow and adventure
forever.
How tragic it would be for us all
if Krishna had lost his flute,
or Lao Tzu had not left his verses
with the gatekeeper for us to find,
or if Mohammed had not listened intently
in his mountain cave.
We too listen for new messages to break forth
from deep within our souls
and attend to those who speak beside us.

Along the way we will hear suffering
in the voices of our cousins far away
and feel it very close in our hearts.
We too sing the human songs of woe and solace.

Along the way we will find joy
leaping in remote villages
and we will delight in our kinship,
feeling a great release for dancing in our hearts.

Along the way we will find an urgency to serve others,
to accomplish peace,
to participate in a larger future
than our own hands alone can build.
May we enlist in the creation
of a just and plenteous future
for all citizens of earth, our cousins.

We find gratitude in our hearts
that we are not all identical in song and vision,
that our humanity has many expressions
for its soul.
May we open ourselves to our multiplicity
of forms and expressions flowing
through the world.
We ask only that in dialogue
we resist not the seeds of transformation
for our lives,
for many voices may speak
to the uniqueness of humanity within us.
As with the sounds of the birds in surrounding trees,
some new melody may take up residence
in our souls,
a new song of life for us to sing
for the morning sun
or the evening moon
on this whirling blue and white planet.

While there is breath in us,
birth and rebirth,
breathing deeply until we die,
may we take up again this journey
with our kinfolk of earth,
giving for all from the melodies of our hearts,
ever giving more to the songs of life,
flowing through us all
in warm embrace of earth.

EARTH SWALLOWED THEM

Earth swallowed them,
men, women, children;
crushed them in their homes,
shook them from sleep to death.

From the red Earth of fields
came the soft brick, from fire
with mud came homes, thatched, snug,
all shaken; returned to Earth again.

Villages, towns, cities
surrounded by red Earth
growing rice, sugar cane, beans, corn,
trees for furniture and fire.

Earth swallowed them,
men, women, children;
crushed them in their homes,
shook them from sleep to death.

From the red Earth came:
barefoot farmers tending fields,
children walking to school,
elders by the old tree with naga steles,
women washing clothes on stones in the stream,
a shepherd squatting near, watching cows,
shopkeepers in sidewalk negotiations,
temple priests in white anointing foreheads,
        assistants cracking coconuts,
mechanics repairing bicycles,
taxi and truck drivers vying for space
        with a bullock-drawn hay wagon.

Earth swallowed them
in quiet time when the moon sinks in the west,
crushed them in their homes,
shook them from sleep to death.

Bus drivers and peddlers
musicians with harmonium, tabula, flute,
dancers who gracefully master movement, form, symbol,
little children who play,
peddlers, magicians, snake charmers,
flower growers, garland weavers --
they have all disappeared
into the Earth, the good and fearsome Earth.

Gentle souls filled with native kindness
        helpful, gracious,
gifted, creative artisans of beauty,
stoical workers, parents, friends
        marking seasons by events,
lovers in embrace of life -
        as the vine entwines the popal tree,
statesmen, bank clerks, policemen, silk merchants,
beggars and mendicants --

Earth swallowed them,
men, women, children;
crushed them in their homes,
shook them from sleep to death.

From the red Earth
comes the bounty of harvest.
From Earth comes birth
        and from Earth comes death.
The terrible snap of rock grinding,
the pouring of bricks upon bodies in the dark,
Earth moves us to terror;
Earth who feeds us, nourishes us,
comforts us in the evening songs of dusk,
rains death upon us in the dawn.

Shock and moaning rises in the morning air,
survivors desperately hoping in rubble.
The song of lament rises in the land.
Music of the temple singers
        takes up the melody of vast ages.

A farmer, barefoot, walks the path to his fields,
finding rice, corn, beans undisturbed -
        reaching for the sun.

Tears come to his eyes as he sinks his hands
into the moist red soil.

Earth swallowed his beloved wife
and his oldest son.
He will build a new house with this same Earth.
He will harvest bounty from this soil.
But in grief there is no speaking of gratitude;
for the good and fearsome Earth
swallowed them before their time,
before the dawn,
and the song of lament hovers
over home and village,
over the fields of life.

LIFE IS NOT FAIR

We did not choose our parents
when we came into the world.
They are who they are:
rich or poor,
Americans or Dominicans or Japanese,
kind and caring,
or perhaps crude or mean spirited.

Our lives may have lengthy or brief duration.
We cannot know more than our mortality,
how long we have,
whether we will be in good health or poor,
lead lives of pain or vigor.

Life is not fair.
The good may or may not prosper.
The transgressor may or may not prosper.
Good fortune only slightly favors the prepared.
Ill fortune only slightly favors the unprepared.

Ill fortune may come out of the blue
in any year, on any day.

In the midst of this unfairness
we seek happiness.
We move towards love
    in our families,
    towards the world.
We enjoy the warmth of the sun
even when we know every attachment,
    every intimate tie,
    shall fall away.

The brevity and unfairness of life
    brings us together.
How else could we find compassion
    in our hearts?
compassion for ourselves,
    for our loved ones?
Compassion for those we meet,
    Compassion for the stranger?

Out of grief and loss
    and the loving ties of our hearts
comes compassion for all living beings:
    in Mozambique,
    in Lawrence,
    and for the companions of our homes.

Compassion must find its action
    to comfort the grieving,
    to encourage the dreams of life
    to bring justice to all.
Compassion brings commitments
    to the center.

In the warmth of this room,
    in the comfort of our circumstances,
    in the brevity of our time here,
reflect upon your compassion.
In the unfairness of life
    look to your actions,
your heart's connection
    to your neighbor.

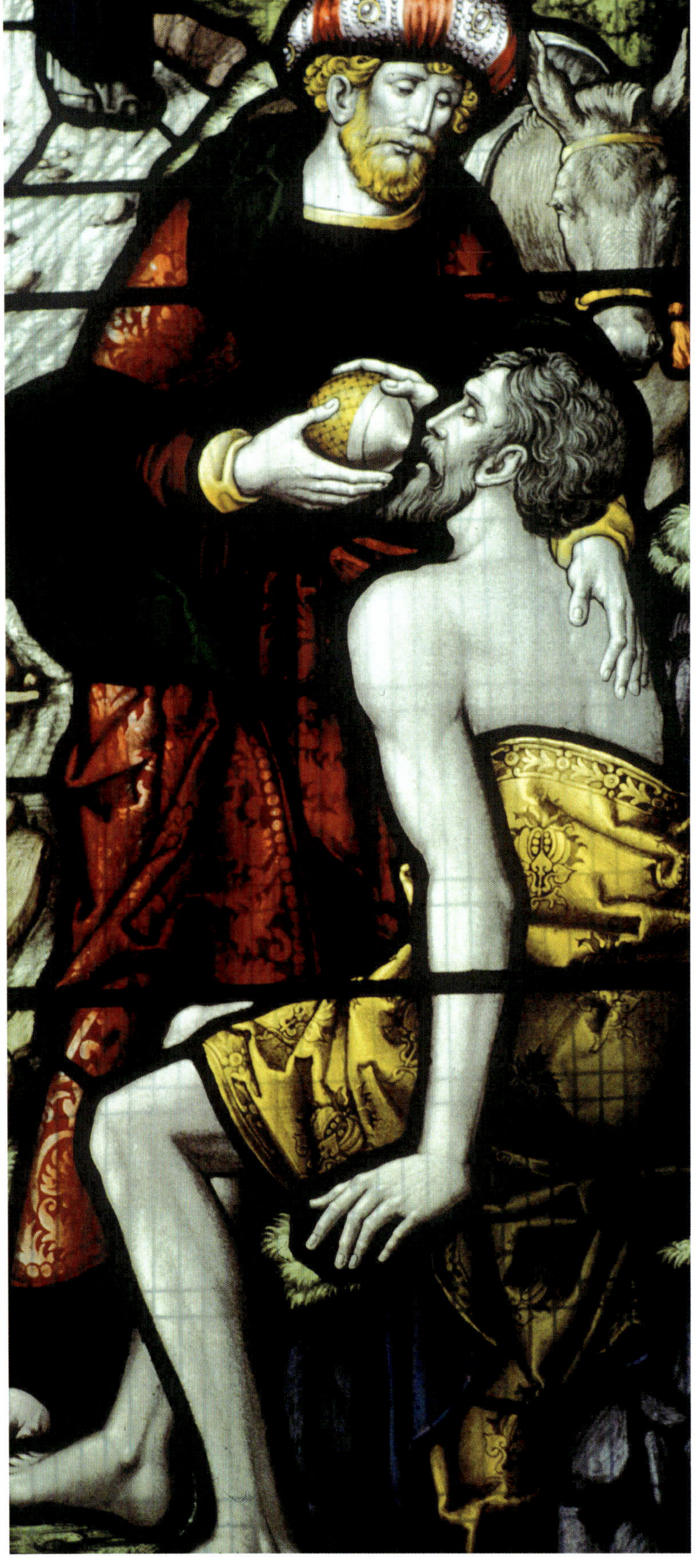

FATIMA

Long ago in a shepherd's family
a little girl tending sheep
found a lamb, lame and bleating.
Her father thought the lamb
would make a good lamb soup
but the girl hugged the lamb,
carried it everywhere,
encouraged the lamb
to take a few faltering steps,
nursed it back to health.

Her name was Fatima.
Not long after, on the way to summer pasture,
Fatima found a boy beside the road,
broken and hungry, abandoned.
He was too weak to walk
and she placed him on the cart
and brought him to her mother's home.
And her heart opened to this child
whose name was Zayd.

This was the beginning
of their love for the world.
They vowed to place their hands upon all pain
beside the highway.
No human want was too great or too small.
A glass of water beside a dusty road
seems a small matter.
Dressing bruised feet
or assisting a person dizzy with sickness
was less common.
But it was not too many months before they realized
more travelers came at noon
when mutton soup was stirring
or at dusk in need of lodging.

The King too stopped to rest his horses.
When he learned they were only poor shepherds
he sent them fifty lambs
and dug for them a new well.
And so passed two lives of kindness
at a dot on the map beside a road
between distant cities.

When they both needed to tend flocks
at summer or winter pasture,
they would leave a trough full of water for horses,
lamb stew simmering for the hungry,
and spare wagon wheels.

Three orphan children were abandoned there
for their care, two girls and a boy.
When Fatima and Zayd grew too old to chase sheep,
these children they loved stepped in for them.

Travelers shared news with them
of many humble dwellings
throughout the Kingdom and beyond
where hospitality had replaced fear,
where highways had become safe,
landscapes kinder for the weary.

When Fatima died in her seventy-first year,
the King and Queen came to stand beside her grave
and the Inman from the grand Mosque
gave prayers of gratitude for the Kingdom.
A field of blue blossoms grew around the site
from flowers left there by travelers.
And in the early dawn
joyful strains of celebration were often heard
from Zayd's flute, mingling with bird songs
in the rising mists and yellow sun beams,
prayerful melodies in the rolling hills of morning.

WATER

Water as fog rolls in from the deep
    past boughs and boats
    surrounding shores, docks, harbor towns.

Fog rises in valleys
    through blades of field grass,
    across country roads,
    obscuring the base of mountains.

Water cascades
    to feed trout and roll round stones,
    only to find a wide winding passage
        back to the sea.

We inhabit a water planet,
    blue, white, green,
    flowing through us;
        every limb and vein
        carried in watery embrace.

Should we be surprised then
    that some journey to Mother Ganges
    to revive the human spirit through immersion
    or to return to the deep?

Should we wonder that Jesus stood in the Jordan
    to receive the dove of heaven;
    Or that Brahma awakened the world
    from the coiled Naga of the primal sea?

STRANGE RESTLESS SIGNS

To the loud chorus of crickets
and cicadas
we invoke the September moon.
What is the song insects lift up
out of the darkness?
What is this late summer song of life,
pulsing, unceasing,
from powdery soil and brown grass
pouring forth sound in the night?

September dawning
brings a more reluctant sun.
Chill lingers
along the morning walk.
We enter a season of appreciation
when patches of sun
fall upon back and arms
to hold us in warm embrace.

The dance of God has begun early
in the maples.
Could it be a warning
of a long November?
Leaves curl quickly
from red to brown
and fall to earth
that is not ready to receive them.
Fruit must ripen
in early fall.

The dance of God brings glory
when earth receives its store
back from the stem
into root.
But it must be moist
for the dance to linger
in full chorus of color.

And seeds must swell in the pod
to fall.
Rain must carry them down
into safe regions
to hold them dark.

The dance of God rattles the maples,
but whirlwinds flow at sea
and tides rip along sand,
waves over ledges.

Strange restless signs
begin this season.
Is there a new star
in the constellations?

We gather to ponder
changes in the cycles,
to consider variations
of life's seasons.

When the God dances
the landscape of life
is transformed.
Each motion outward
brings counter waves
of restoration
in wholeness of being.
Enjoy the whirling dance
and the balance of earth.

HEARTH-SIDE HORRORS

Tuesday, perhaps at 3 or 4 in the morning
a dream came forth in the dark.
I was in front of a fireplace
in which no fire was burning.
My amplifier was on the hearth.
I reached my hand to turn a dial,
pulled back with a jolt
but it was not an electric shock.
It was burning heat on flesh.
Below the hearth bricks
was a boiling sea of fire.

I sprang out of bed.
Shaken I walked downstairs,
drank a glass of cooling water,
rolled back into bed in the dark.

A few hours later jetliners
vaporized into boiling flames.
Buildings dissolved.
There was no refuge,
no solace at the hearth.

Before: I viewed the twin towers
of the World Trade Center
only from the harbor, far away.
I have never walked beneath them
nor ascended their 110 stories,
had any reason to do so
nor any desire to do so.

Now: I encountered the towers again
in images of terror from afar,
horrendous nightmare images
of burning flesh, crushed limbs, screams,
clouds of lethal dust boiling in the dark.

I hope never again
to see a jetliner
disappear into a sea of glass
transformed into a sphere of flame
out of the blue.

Finally the rains came.
After four days, the skies opened
and water descended
upon the dusty streets,
the bruised buildings,

the frantic firemen digging for comrades,
the still glowing broken beams of steel;
upon widows, widowers, orphans,
the gentle rains descended.

There is no comfort at the hearth;
information media cannot console
the grieving heart.
Only the rain can cool
the startled fearful jolt,
the awakened dread.
Finally the rains came
a sign from gathering clouds
of hope.

KOL NIDRE

The lamp is lit.
The scroll is opened in the Book of Life.
The sound of spiritual alarm is heard in the depths.

What promises remain unkept
as we gaze at the bright sky?
Life warming sun enfolds us.
But our pact with earth
rests heavy in unfaithful hearts.

The lamp is lit.
The scroll is opened in the Book of Life.
The sound of spiritual alarm is heard in the depths.

Our covenant with grandparents
        rests in forgotten silence.
And our parents wait patiently
        for encouraging word and deed
        to boost their spirits.
Days of busyness
obscure our gratitude.

Who can discern needs of children,
independent in new formed households,
or the expectancy of little grandchildren,
ready to laugh and run circles for doting elders.
Life moves on, and away
from those who hesitate, and recedes from view.

The lamp is lit.
The scroll is opened in the Book of Life.
The sound of spiritual alarm is heard in the depths.

Our vows of union and life commitment grow old
        in comfortable living.
Our partners must assume our love
        unspoken, unheralded in gestures of celebration.

Friends far away forget our names,
        so distant has been our silence.
Near at hand, friends wait kindly
        as we forget to respond to their overtures of care.

The lamp is lit.
The scroll is opened in the Book of Life.
The sound of spiritual alarm is heard in the depths.

We promised ourselves quiet times
in which to dream restorative affirmations,
        forgotten promises.

We vowed exercise, nutrition, rest
to strengthen tired places,
        forgotten vows.
Adventures, and projects won, we envisioned,
but we continue as before.

The lamp is lit.
The scroll is opened in the Book of Life.
The sound of spiritual alarm is heard in the depths.

The circle of the seasons
        hastens into autumn.
The barns are full, the houses warm,
but we have not prepared our minds
        for the dying of the year.
Autumn cannot enter the preoccupied heart.

What inertia keeps us from action?
What demons may distract attention
        from humane and gentle resolution?
What preoccupations assume control
        while the issues of life languish?
The moment on the compass nears
        for repentance.

The lamp is soon extinguished.
The scroll is sealed in the Book of Life.
The sound of spiritual alarm is still remembered in the depths.

AUTUMN MEETING

It was a glorious autumn day
bright blue deep sky
falling brilliant upon golden leaves
remaining on maple limbs
with writhing trunk
rooting into earth.

Beneath that tree
far across the green
was an afternoon bench
and upon it a figure bent
basking in contemplation.

In fixation drawn
as if to some fateful meeting,
footfalls hardly meeting ground,
I crossed
into this silence.

He was there, bowed,
looking ahead past me
to the hillside beyond
from where I had journeyed.

He looked rather gray,
tightened skin
lined about the eyes and mouth,
roostered neck
surrounded by worn shirt
and buttoned sweater.

As I took a place beside him
his face fell into an inviting smile
of cordial welcome,
even while he seemed conflicted
whether to engage in pleasantries
or to continue melting his gaze
into the hillside beyond.

The sun had baked this spot
raising an odor from skin
old people sometimes carry
when washing hurts.
His beard was a day or two grown.

We spoke pleasantries
of trees and sun,
the good fortune of living

vibrant in such a world,
brilliant, transient, laden
with colors flowing
into the autumn earth.

He did not notice
two golden leaves
which fell upon wisps of hair
remaining on his head,
as another rested briefly
on his shoulder
stooped towards earth.

His breathing was easy,
deep and rhythmic,
as his hand shook
when raised from his knee.
I couldn't be sure he heard
every word spoken,
only the general intention
of its meaning.

It was a good meeting
in this autumn interlude
before November, before the long cold.
I felt a quiet joy
falling like a breeze under the sun.
I rose to leave
with two golden leaves on my head,
when a third fell from my shoulder
upon the ground.

A STRANGE WONDERMENT

Yesterday as I was driving
I saw two grey squirrels
in the middle of the street.
One was on its back, its four feet up,
its head flattened red on the pavement.
The other sat there beside
on its hind legs.

As I approached the living squirrel
scampered into the bushes
leaving me with a strange wonderment
in my heart.

This was the third grey squirrel
killed on our street this month.
They are so busy scampering
for nuts and seeds
they have lost their usual caution
about crossing the street.

But never before have I seen
one squirrel stop and stare
at death. Never before
have I seen one keep vigil.

A tiny grey squirrel
does not know as we know
about the loneliness
of the long winter ahead.

A tiny grey squirrel
does not anticipate as we do
its own demise

when it finds its companion
dead in the street.

Was it a brother or sister,
a parent, a mate,
or just a passing cousin
curious at the smell of death,
to find no pulse of life.

What can a tiny grey squirrel
know of love or of grief?
What apprehension
caused its pausing, its vigil,
on the centerline of my street?

Whatever its tinge of recognition
enters perhaps from another dimension,
one which eventually
finds us.

All I know is -
I have never seen
a grey squirrel pause
in vigil
beside a dead companion.

Perhaps I project grief
in a scene warranting only
passing curiosity.

After all, I imagine
songbirds call for me
when the bird feeder is empty
and sing for me
when it is full.

I'm being silly.
They always startle
and fly away
when I approach.

But I do have
a strange wonderment
in my heart.

TO HOLD DEEP SHADOWS CLOSE

for Samhain

A shudder contracts the shoulder blades
as the season's first chill
shakes loose apprehensions
of approaching winter.

Before us are the inexorable seasons
of autumn and the long night.
We know where we are
following birth, youth, fruitfulness;
without mercy, the spiral motion of the seasons
for an indifferent span.

The long descent into subterranean Earth
has begun, beneath the cold
into nether regions,
the good and wise return.

Dried leaves rattle
like skulls around the neck of the goddess
to be absorbed into earth
as a chorus of late October winds
swirls sounds of desolation.

Squirrels gather nuts, frantically scurrying
to store supply for a deep cold winter.
One squirrel, injured by a car
rests in agony beside the road in the grass.
A black carrion crow
lands on a low limb, watching,
the dark void of death
reflected in bright beady eyes.

Hearing death is part of life
does not lighten our fear
of its hold.

A winter that endures past any spring
brings up images of rooms below,
ghosts in the fissures,
apparitions in the garden twilight.
Have you not been jolted into recognition
of a vanished loved one coming through --
a glimpse in the gray revolving sidewalk carousel?

If we could only know,
see past the veil,
into the darkness numinous:
To hear cadence of my grandmother's voice again;
To feel my child hand in my grandfather's;
To ask my younger brother if it matters dying young,
now;
To ask my second wife if cheerful greetings,
        all the tangibles of graphic art
        or of fresh cut flowers on trestle tables past
        matters now.
If only I could renew all the stories
        that once were so clear
        in my great aunt's voice;
Or catch my father's eye
        for an accounting,
        even a silent approval.

Would such a visit in the presence of loved ones
leave any solace for this life?
Perhaps it is enough to hold
deep shadows close.

(Leaves turn brilliant red and fall,
The crow appears on yet another limb,
We can hear the rattling of Kali's skulls,
Memories quietly fade,
The veil is numinous.
With a sigh we return
to prepare for another winter.)

FAR MORE THAN MEETS THE EYE

There is far more in our lives
than meets the eye.
We live in a small part
of all which we know.
Beneath our conscious existence
stretches a vast universe
of human experience, emerging
from fathomless time.

There is far more
than meets the eye:
beyond horizons of Earth's
atmosphere,
beyond where gravity's pull
is lightened,
great systems open
in outer space.

There is far more
than meets the eye.
Within the brain
are endless dendrites
stretching further
than the Milky Way;
and behind the brain,
the mind.

There is far more
than meets the eye
in simple human feeling,
in love.
The gaze of the lover
upon the beloved

carries numberless waves
	of awareness, in time.
There is far more
	than meets the eye
as a mountain stream
	flows smoothly
like ribbon candy,
	one continuous band
of water folding
	over rocks innumerable.

There is far more
	than meets the eye.
Leaves turning brilliant
	into burning orange,
falling into currents of wind,
	carried, churning,
are crushed beneath feet
	into numberless grains of soil.

There is far more
	than meets the eye.
Through the southern window
	pours a yellow beam of sunlight.
Children know this transformation
	of the unseen,
gazing in rapt fascination
	at millions of dust motes whirling.

There is far more
	than meets the eye
when the human voice
	sings alleluia,
the breath flowing along
	inward passages
and the song flowing
	through cadences of melody.

There is far more in our lives
	than meets the eye.
Who can imagine
	the emergence of God,
beyond the flow
	of gratitude,
beyond evolution
	or even love?

HUNTERS' MOON

Hunters' moon is full
to soothe the wounds of fall,
embracing trees
bereft of leaves
waving light across blades of grass
about to brown.

The tide of life recedes
as cycles of insect,
amphibian, bird, retreat
into the somber hush
of abandoned limbs and nests,
cooling waters and turf.

A season for grief
waves through the landscape,
a time for parting
from summer's comforts.
Lamentations cover silver shadows
as a dog brays mournfully.

The orange maple beside the road
is already bare in its crown.
Skeleton limbs stretch
into a gray sky
revealing large crows
Silhouetted in the moon's orb.

When it is still night
hunters prepare
to take up their stations
for the morning's kill,
thinning the herd before winter's cold,
adding venison to the harvest.

At the shore against ledges
waves curl and crash
while as far as the eye can see,
is pale reflected light upon rolling water,
and the sound of gulls mocking
across eternal tides.

The grateful heart
remembers the harvest,
pauses for a lifetime more, serene,
to contemplate one fallen leaf,
breathes deeply of the cooling air
to admire a stark and stately moon.

CHILDREN REMEMBER

I.

I remember attending five Sunday schools:
Congregational, Presbyterian, Methodist and Baptist.
My parents may have flirted also with the Episcopalians
except that incense and kneeling were out of range for
my father's sense of propriety.
My mother objected on intellectual grounds.
The others depended more on the personality of the
minister, though the Presbyterians were a bit heavy
handed on matters of doctrine for my mother.

I remember very little of spaces or people in the early
years. I cannot recall a single church school room,
although I vaguely feel they were mostly subterranean.
It was qualities that remain with me,
    qualities of friendliness and acceptance,
    of genuine interest, care and love --
    grandmotherly qualities.

After fourth grade I remember Mr. Baker.
    He was huge with big worker's hands.
    He delivered oil to our house in his truck.
    He would tell Old Testament stories
        in a loud and dramatic voice
        that could be exciting.
When my great aunt gave me Egermeier's Bible Story
Book on Easter Sunday
    I read all these stories again.

The only other teacher I remember was my mother's best friend, Jinny Dodge.

She was resourceful and had a silly laugh.
Everything was infectiously enjoyable.

They were quite a team and ran Vacation Bible School.
We memorized:

the books of the Bible
the Ten Commandments
Psalms 1,23,and 121
Micah 6:8
the Beatitudes
the Lord's Prayer
the Golden Rule
the Great Commandment.

When I reached the age of reason, I took a class with the minister, Mr. Maxfield, to prepare for Baptism. It was after this experience that orthodoxy and I parted company.

II.

What will our children remember about us?

I hope they will enjoy being in church and feel it to be their home.

I hope they will meet people who are friendly and welcoming, who speak their names, who affirm them, care about them and love them.

I hope they will sing songs of the gods and goddesses, of the male and female spiritual qualities, of the beauty and majesty of nature, of the reliable warmth of the sun, the resilient bounty of the earth, of courage, goodness and gratitude.

I hope they will hear wonderful stories of Jacob and Joseph, of the prophets Micah and Elijah, of Moses, Jesus, the Buddha and an old man who rode a water buffalo through the gate and handed the gatekeeper his Tao te Ching.

I hope they will learn poetry and wisdom so that when they grow very old, and forget all else, they will be able to fill the air with beautiful thoughts.

I hope they will remember one or two of us, how we laughed, the way we spoke or used our hands, the reality of our devotion to the posterity of life and tangibly to them.

MOBILIZE FOR WOMEN'S LIVES

God of us all:
At this sunrise of a new day
we gather to announce a great wave of freedom
to awaken a continent.

We announce the freedom of women equal with men:
equal in their humanity,
equal in their power as spiritual beings
to enlist their faculties
of mind and body, heart and soul,
as agents of free moral choice.

We are here, O God, to raise our voices in affirmation
of the right of women, as free responsible persons,
to decide whether or not, and when
the time is right,
to enter the sacred duties of motherhood,
to nurture the birth and growing of a new
spiritual being,
to welcome with a joyous and grateful heart
the parental bond.
We know, O God, that we are free spiritual beings,
that there is no law in the heavens or on earth
which can dictate that choice
which we are created to make for ourselves.

We witness here today to that dearest right
of all individuals to make their private choices
concerning their own bodies
concerning those moral and religious beliefs
that will guide their living.

And we announce, this morning,
our sense of compassion for all women who suffer,
whose lives have been taken from them
and given to forces which enslave the human spirit.
We speak to the condition of all
who are burdened in poverty or despair,
who are abandoned by the careless, the self-righteous,
    by those who do violence to the human spirit,
    and by those who do not know the social costs
    of spiritual hypocrisy and intolerance.
We pause for all who suffer
    because this day took so long to dawn
    upon our hearts.

May this sunrise of a new day
bring freedom closer for all our sisters and brothers,
and may every child that is born into the world
be a wanted child:
welcomed, loved, given sustenance and opportunity
to come into their full humanity.

God of all:
Strengthen us for this new day of freedom,
for the centrality of our human right to choose.
Bring us into our destiny as spiritual beings.

Amen.

FOR THE SHARING OF BREAD

The circle is the oldest form
    for religious celebration.

It is the community gathered
    where every individual is present
    for all others in the circle.

Bread is the gift of life,
    baked from grains of earth,
    universal symbol of the animation of life.

Even as yeast animates
    and expands to create the loaf.

So also shall our love for each other
    grow to embrace this circle
    and the world we serve beyond.

Therefore do we break this bread
to share with each other
around this circle,

even as we share our lives
and nurture our common life,
one with another.

NOVEMBER HARVEST

The cold came in last night,
the November cold.
The chill blew through trees.
It rattled berries left in bushes.
Frost stiffened the ground.
November is no time for harvest.

When we hear November winds
it is a drama of the turning season.
When sounds bounce off hard ground
there is no life left in the soil.
When the barren landscape portends
harsh winter to follow,
we retreat within
to warm circles of our gathering.

November mocks growing life.
It chases dead leaves into hiding.
All harvest bounty is stored
secure in barns and cellars.
Only gratitude remains
to still the storms of warning.

What else but Thanksgiving remains for us
when November hardens the world?
What else but a circle of gratitude
can warm our hearts?
Secure in our common store to sustain us,
in defiance of all cold winds,
we share our harvest bread together

THANKSGIVING

I.

When Pilgrims came to these shores
they found windswept snow
on cold hard soil.
They found deep untracked forests,
frozen streams,
an indian cache of dried corn
and set about building a common house.

This continent has favored us with prosperity.
We live in shiny insulated houses
heated with oil and electricity.
We command great chains of supply
brought to us by thousands of hands,
while around us sweeps the same desolate cold
over hard soil.

May we remember,
God of our gratitude,
that we live because others persisted
through all obstacles
to give us life.
May we pause to become more aware
that the relative prosperity
we have inherited
is not shared by all who inhabit this brown land,
that there are those in our midst
who inhabit November homes
not unlike the common house
in which half the Pilgrims died
in the winter of 1620.

II.

The air is chill
when New England gives thanks
The food of the harvest meal
is brown, gold, red, orange.
It is a harvest dried in fields
and hung in barns for a long storage.
It is a feast not of luxury
but of gratitude.

The Pilgrims had little;
they were not certain it would last them
through the winter ahead.
But there was an inner need
to express to the cold landscape
to the long season before them
a song of the human spirit
a song which sings in all conditions
its gratitude for life.
There is a willfulness of inner strength
that takes dried kernels of corn
and crushed cranberries
and venison the Indians brought,
holds them up
and marshals 100 voices
at the edge of winter
to sing Thanksgiving!

And thus do we pause here this morning,
a few in the midst of many;
we pause to affirm life
in the midst of this community.
We dedicate ourselves to become Pilgrims
to fashion anew a world for life,
a new resilience on this continent,
on this planet spinning in dark space
a new persistence,
a Pilgrim warmth.
We pause in the stillness
to awaken once again
Pilgrim songs that take all the browns, golds,
reds and oranges
in this wind swept landscape,
the deep themes of Thanksgiving,
for a new beginning.

AS A LAKSHMI LAMP

for Divali

I.

The tree is felled
cut, split,
kindled upon the altar.

Fatted calf, mutton,
dove or rabbit,
is roasted on the flames.

The smoke of sacrifice ascends,
one pillar spiraling
linking earth and sky as one.

A family gives to the gods
the largest portion of livelihood
in gratitude for life.

II.

Lakshmi holds a votive lamp
tilted perfectly to feed oil
to a lighted wick.

She stands patient
in posture perfect
to proffer steady light.

Not one drop can be lost
not one ripple in the oil
can be loosed to compromise the flame.

A steady light burns
to light the altar
until it is wholly given up.

So too we live to give,
carefully gathering together our store of good,
to spend at the altar of life.

III.

May we guard closely
that store of goodness, truth, and beauty
we have gleaned in the harvest.

May we give intensely, fully,
to the altar of our calling,
yielding a steady flame.

May we stand before the altar
with pure integrity of devotion
abundant love in our hearts.

May the unique flame of our offering
burn brightly, generous,
offering all to life, until all is given.

MACCABEUS

Mattathias, the old priest,
in his last passion,
exhorted his sons to risk all,
their blood and soul,
to cleanse the altar
of their God.

And John, Simon, Eleazar,
Jonathan and Judas Maccabeus
all died by the sword.

They formed armies,
fearlessly defeated hordes brought against them,
plundered, burned villages, intrigued,
massacred thousands,
to gain national freedom.

And John, Simon, Eleazar,
Jonathan and Judas Maccabeus
all died by the sword.

They stormed the temple,
slaughtered false priests,
removed bloody stones
and abominations
and made the temple bright again.

They gained a place
to practice their faith,
coerced all who remained
to keep the holy law,
executed all dissent.

And John, Simon, Eleazar,
Jonathan and Judas Maccabeus
all died by the sword.

They formed a close loyalty
to honor their covenant
made long ago in the desert,
moved as one body,
a ‘saving remnant’ for truth
and righteousness.

Feeling alone in a sea of dissent
they built fortresses.
All faith and belief was examined at the door.
Only those who understood

could cross the treshold.
Most who applied were refused, told to wait
out on the unprotected plain.

And John, Simon, Eleazar,
Jonathan and Judas Maccabeus
all died by the sword.

The solitary mind,
the autonomous character,
the self reliant individual,
the questioner,
the pilgrim in search
of the unknown and mysterious,
new visions and aspirations,
to them was unknown.

And John, Simon, Eleazar,
Jonathan and Judas Maccabeus
all died by the sword.

But they kindled a bright light,
they polished menorahs
and burned sacred oil,
they gazed at the flame
certain that it had meaning
somehow beyond what they knew,
beyond even their passion.

And John, Simon, Eleazar,
Jonathan and Judas Maccabeus
all died by the sword.

The light was beyond their means
and beyond their meanness.
It probed the darkness,
beyond knowing,
beyond capture or coercion,
beyond any grasp or strategy,
beyond earth, beyond breathing.

And John, Simon, Eleazar,
Jonathan and Judas Maccabeus
all died by the sword,
living the questions
others would ask,
in the dim range of gentle light
life holds out into the darkness.

A DARK TIME

It is a dark time
　　　　dark when we rise in the morning,
　　　　dark when we travel in late afternoon.
Day fades to night
　　　　And there is a great wintry darkness.

I cannot explain the intensity
　　　　of this coming together
　　　　the dark inspires.
We cannot take our daylight
　　　　for granted.
We hesitate to venture far
　　　　to insure our return to safety.
We seek out the company of others
　　　　in family, in community.
Lighting candles, kindling fires,
　　　　we stare at flames leaping,
tongues stretching the light
　　　　through the dark.

In summer light I felt no concern
to extend the day
but welcomed the dark for rest
to complement plenteous light.
In the long days of summer I traveled to distant places.
I wandered freely from early morning
to late evening in the light.
To be individual was enough,
to explore, to grow, to adventure.

But as the light recedes
thoughts turn to gathering with companions
for comfort and assurance
against the dark.
I am not daring when cold could freeze
and dark conceal my whereabouts from rescue.
Dark constrains
drives us inward
concentrates community.
We gather, telling stories around the fire
to concentrate warmth around the light,
keeping at bay surrounding cold..

At the Nadir of the sun
winter has furthest extended confining gloom.
Winter begins in its greatest darkness.
The draining of the light will cease.
The sun is reborn in a dark time.
Winter is lived with hope returning.

Gather for the holidays
to light lamps.
Gather to welcome the returning sun,
the promise of the solstice.
Gather intensely to kindle faith
to live the return of light
through cold months of lengthening day.

GOLDEN SEED

Quiet ground awaits,
frozen seed held hard
beneath the snow,
for the Sun's birth.

Earth's cave
cradles an infant,
innocent, peaceful
in warm glow
of Sun's gold.

When the oak
surrendered its leaves,
and lost limbs
in winter storms,
torn in grief
it rested.

The newborn
knows nothing of cold winds,
of wounds suffered
for living,
endurance through
all inhospitable forces.

Following light
in the spangled sky,
cozy with kings,
magi inadvertently
nearly killed life's prospect.

Shepherds awestruck
adored the child,
oblivious to dangers,
simple folk, ineffectual
towards evil.

The night sky blazoned
in a million cold lights
penetrated to the heart
of barren earth and snow
a complete indifference.

Only Mary and Joseph
could protect this haloed life,
hold it warm,
give it refuge
until its time

to open the world
for its springtime.

When snow is deep
and night bears in, brutal,
it is pointless to disturb
the seed of life.

Prepare the soul
by the flames
of solstice fires.
Let it lie golden
for its spring.

BLINKING LIGHTS ON A BARE TREE

In a time of grief I beheld
blinking lights on a bare tree
against a beige colored house.

Not uncommon, those tiniest of lights,
red, green, yellow, blue, white,
on a small tree
next to a homely house.

But I came upon them
at a tender time
of fatherless loss.

It just seemed glorious,
the exhaltation
of the bare and barren tree
against a plastic wall.

In December, I know
leaves will sometime reappear
and fragrant blossoms,
that life simmers thick below.

But in a season of joy
when death hangs upon the landscape
my grateful heart beheld
blinking lights on a bare tree
against a beige colored house.

I don't know if anyone else could see
just what I found there
in the soft darkening dusk,
twinkling colored lights
on the tree of life.

God dwells in those lights
pulsing on brittle branches,
bringing life to death,
color in monochromed light.

I saw them only once,
felt their comfort in my surprise
and forgot to look again
a dozen more times
after the veil closed
in my attention.

For days now, on an inner canvass,
I have found tender recollections
of blinking lights on a bare tree
against a beige colored house.

MIDNIGHT MASS

Eleanor has her Christmas presents
    all wrapped and labeled.
She tells me not to buy more wrapping paper.
There is plenty left.
I hope she is right
    for I never wrap presents
    until midnight, Christmas Eve.

First I like to write my sermon
    for Christmas Sunday.
Next I fuss over Christmas Eve.
I am quite attached to Christmas Eve,
    the candles and singing in the night.

After that, when the adrenaline subsides back home,
I settle into a semiconscious state.

Only then do thoughts turn to wrapping presents.
I always wrap in front of the television set
tuned into Midnight Mass
at St. Peter's Basilica in Rome.
Yes, that is when I wrap presents.

Now why would a Unitarian Universalist,
a minister no less,
one who has preached extensively
on the contrast of orthodoxies
with his own approach on the spiritual journey,
watch old men process
and crowds stand in awe
in the largest church in Christendom?

Well, I don't really know.
Once I tuned in early

and heard an amazing black choir
in New York City.
Another time I witnessed
a large Protestant service with choirs,
readings, prayers and even a homily,
in a Congregational church in Connecticut.
But I stayed tuned until midnight
for St. Peter's in Rome.

One time I fell asleep
and woke up after static had replaced
the last "venite adoramus."
But my tradition continues
honored or understood by no one else I know.
I just tune in the Vatican
and let it wash over my mellowed out
holiday self.

The only irritation is the commentary,
the same old soto-voice each year
explaining what is going on.
I would just as soon not know.
It suffices to see the four huge serpentine
baroque pillars,
and the marble altar,
with candles, sacred liturgical books,
silver goblets of wine, silver plates with wafers,
the pot on a chain waving clouds of incense,
and priests taking off and putting on
hats and vestments.
I soak in high wavering voices speaking sacred words
in multiple languages.

Yes, I probably should plan my life better,
wrap the presents days early,
after Christmas Eve enjoy a drink of water,
go to bed, and sleep.
Why push the envelope,
leave all this to the last minute,
and for an hour or two
witness pious crowds
and devout words
half a world away?
I don't know.
And I have ceased to ask why.
That is just what I do
year after year.
I look forward to midnight tomorrow
and my annual pilgrimage to Rome.

WINTER APPLE TREE

There is another kind of "Peace on Earth."
It comes toward us across the landscape
to touch something quiet within us.

I saw an old apple tree beside the turnpike
fully formed, scarred, proud,
twisting, branching, as only apple trees do,
outlined with December snow.

It was a cleared space
before the forest began
It was alone, abandoned, itself
with a dark forest and a calm field
in winter stillness.

Perhaps a house once stood
where my car now speeds by.
Perhaps there was a barn and shed,
a dooryard well,
an orchard planted
to keep this solitary tree company.

I wonder what human voices once stirred the air?
What children climbed up through your limbs?

What plantings and harvests surrounded you?
What enjoyments, family reunions, snow shoeing trails?
What sounds and smells and sights of habitation?

You now stand a stranger
between forest and road.
Now it is the fumes of diesel and gasoline,
the engulfing forest, the quiet clearing,
a brave isolation.

Why did the woodcutters spare you?
Because you could not make lumber?
Were too much bother to burn?

So now you live on,
your pretty blossoms unplucked in spring,
your apples falling unwanted in autumn,
your branches unpruned
holding powdery filigrees of snow,
grey and white sentinal,
messenger of times' changing landscapes,
helping a passing romantic at 60 mph
connect with your past
of homes and livelihoods,
of joys and sorrows long ago.

A quietness descends
tree and person held transfixed.
A silent gift is given, a landscape reflecting
meanings magically personal,
meanings we all have
in a cherished place
inside.

IN THE PAUSING TIME

Ice and the darkness rule
as life ebbs from the old year.
Extremities grow cold, waiting,
in the pausing time
for New Year's birth.

Memories hover
for the year's living:
nostalgia for good times,
regret for disappointments,
reflection for meanings.
Hesitation is neutral
in the gray landscape
of the year's last day.

The old and the new
converge in this silence,
weighing the balance
for our action,
for our being in itself,
for influences radiating
from these hands, heart, soul,
out through light and darkness.

In fullness of time
this life, this year
in readiness, can be released,
allowed to float
into the western hills
dark, lost in cool haze.

Why retain remnants of life
drifting into bitterness?

Why grow attached to pain,
to regrets,
when memory has loves, outlived,
has followed all adventures
born of hope,
has held experience, rounded
in its fullness, complete?

The snow falls gentle
through bare branches
of tired winter's worn nadir.
For the elder in patient waiting
dusk brings a quiet defeat
accepting the embrace of long night.

It is benign in the dawn
bequeathing new beginnings.
The year opens in absence,
new life longing
warm in the eastern glow.

DREAMS/RESOLUTIONS

On the first night
of the New Year
I dreamed an earthquake
collapsed a stone church
onto my younger daughter
when she was only a toddler.
I crawled in through the rubble
to where she was trapped.
Her little arm was showing
and I felt her pulse beating.

The picture was so disturbing
it woke me up.
I don't know how it would resolve.
I don't know what it means.

On the second night
of the New Year

I dreamed I was to give a lecture
but I forgot one thing.
So I headed to my room;
down hallways, stairways,
across a lawn.
A five minute walk
took hours!

I was late.
I ran down
hallways after hallways,
turned corners
into still more hallways,
running to keep my appointment
but I couldn't get back.

On the third night
of the New Year,
I didn't sleep.
I didn't dream.

I wrestled with a sermon
that kept refusing to jell,
a nightmare of a different sort
to keep one awake!

New Year's resolutions!
To do yoga practice.
To write.
To organize.
To keep in touch with family
            and parishioners.
To turn off the TV.
Sensible, ambitious
            resolutions,
to care for body, emotions,
            mind and soul.

May we protect, streamline,
order our lives.
May we resolve goals,
achievements.

But our dreams,
may we receive them
as gifts from the great chaos
to awaken order
to larger possibilities.

TO BUILD AND TO BUILD AGAIN

When I was a child I waited for the big storm.
I would take my shovel and build a large pile of packed snow.
Then I would hollow it out.
Inside would be a cozy room:
quiet, sheltered,
gleaming blue white all around me.

After several hours I would be wet and cold
and would abandon my shelter
for the house and a hot tub.
Sometimes when I was not looking
other children would crash my shelter to pieces
and the gleaming blue white
would be broken pieces and overshoe tracks.

My mother assured me the world had two kinds of people:
the builders and the destroyers,
the trusting and the jealous,
and I was a builder.

The snow of the big storm
brings us together.
In the gleaming blue white walls of winter
we can build our lives inside.
We can come together
sheltered from the cold.
We can be builders, not destroyers.
We can be trusting and not jealous.

We can be who we are,
when every storm comes upon us,
walking into the outdoors, shovel in hand,
trusting, to build
and to build again.

WHERE IS GOD?

Earth holds to itself
the riches of the ages,
the dark loam of life.

Trees crashing to the ground,
    proud trunks and bark,
    limbs graceful, delicate leaves,
all pulverized into soil.

The gentle deer
bounding across a field
over a bush and into the jaws of a wolf,
lies broken, torn, absorbed.

Like the snap of a scorpion
    by night
or the fangs of a rattle snake by day,
the very ground we walk upon
    can suddenly burst open in danger.

The Serbian Orthodox mass was celebrated,
Divine mysteries profound,
while in the next village
cousins bulldozed a thousand-year old mosque.

And in Tibet, lamas,
in prayer sequences
spoken thousands of years ago,
are herded outside
and shot in heaps.

Through all this journey
    we aspire to reach God.
This carnage is too unpleasant to contemplate
    but grabs us about the ankles.

When will the great transformation begin,
    the ascension into heaven?

When will there be no hands with weapons
  no hearts raging with revenge?

Not in our lifetimes will we see heavens
  come to earth.
There can be no shortcut
  for this journey of countless ages.

We can only look to our hearts
  firmly mend, gently love,
in the pathways of our living
  for those we know.

We can build up our affiliations
  beyond the familial,
embrace humanity and life beyond
  in universal kinship.

Where is God
  in a world of war and starvation?
For now fill your mind with the wonder of starlight
  and the beating of your heart.
Face into the abundance of life.
  Make your choices resolutely.
Anticipate springtime beneath the snow.

JESUS COULD NOT HAVE WALKED

Jesus could not have walked
in sandled feet
through New England's winters.

He could not have sailed
New England's ships
with Beatitudes of peace.

He could not have spoken
of the good shepherd
when island sheep grazed unattended.

With no visible means of income
few would have listened
or provided meal or friendship.

New England is a cool place
where hearth fire and quill pen
come before a hearing.

In New England one's calling
must yield visible signs
of prudential rewards on earth.

The Kingdom of Heaven on earth
required a well stocked barn
and a Sunday suit.

But here too we suffer
grief, losses of life
to the sea and field.

Here too in swirling snows
when the hearth coals cool
loneliness chills along the spine.

Here in villages and across hills
life's ennui can nag
when the joys fade into routine.

Here love needs rekindling,
sympathy, neighbor for neighbor,
must brave winter's ice.

Into villages we converge,
into plain rooms for worship
to speak each other's names.

Into circles for singing and speaking,
        rugged individuals join hands
to greet the week's first day.

Into gatherings for quiet reflection
        there are always friends to notice
who is present and who is absent.

Many years of congregational connection
        experiences together, overcomes reticence,
the faltering spirit meets a warm embrace.

Jesus could not have walked here
        but some presence of his memory
springs resilient through New England's heart.

PRUNING THE APPLE TREE

Universal dampness of earth,
frost melting to soften the ground,
I could hear the bubbles
around the soles of my shoes
as I sank a ladder into the sod
and rested it upon the gnarled trunk
of an ancient sweet apple tree.

It was too warm
for the last day of February.
The annual pruning must be done.
This tree, hollow in all its large limbs,
sends up shoots aimed straight at the sun's zenith,
hundreds of them weighing down
on that aged trunk.

The tree rises like some monster of the deep
through writhing dragon forms
of elegant southward leanings
that defy earth's gravity
while at the top a thousand twigs
long for union with the sun.

A family of red squirrels
occupy a mile of tunnels inside.
Close to the ground beneath the lowest den
water seeps through from rotting dampness within.

So there is an urgency to preserve
this ancient living form
against the ravages of time,
to keep it sunward
unabsorbed and above
embrace of ground.

Firewood and ashes
could not satisfy the eye
which caresses each
undulating flaming limb.

So forgive me sweet apple tree
for two hundred wounds
on your crown, to save you
for the sun and for the soul
of he who watches for first green
a month or two from now.

YEAR 4693

A February storm:
wind roaring,
snow-rain-sleet transforming,
cold flowing through trees,
over ledges,
around us gathered
warm inside.

Circle of remembrance:
honoring a deep past
lived with two friends,
a feeling of loss
that haunts and builds in the emptiness
a tragic, compassionate awareness
that is the beginning of wisdom.

And the New Year's dragon
darting, undulating, thrusting through,
connecting chi powers,
playful, exulting, random joy,
our laughter, our fear, anticipations.
A poke in the rib !
Mystic insight !
A far journey ! A near miss !
New energy breaks out!

Families gather here:
two partners, single households,
parents with children,
families broken, dispersed or isolated,
families close, connected in wide circles.
All come to this place
with a longing in their hearts
to reach out beyond themselves,
to experience the wider kinship
of our humanity (jen).

Keep your feet on the ground
in the "five blessings" of year 4693.
We wish them for our elders,
we wish them for our children,
our parents, our friends:
- "longevity" to live a full life,
all four seasons of our lifetime,
to bring things to fruition,
to see how things turn out.
- "wealth" enough to support
and sustain a good life,
to prosper a whole household.
- "health" physical, mental, spiritual well-being.

- "love of virtue" to live with a humane substance:
  in the (Confucian) virtues
  of benevolence, justice, propriety, wisdom,
  sincerity,
  that the world will be transformed
  and brought into harmony for all.
- to die "a natural death,"
  to be captain of one's ship to the end,
  to have the company of loving
  family and friends
  in the last moments,
  to be remembered in a circle
  of continuity and meaning.

Keep your feet on the ground
but keep walking:
into deep forest glens
and along craggy pathways
through mountains.
Sit on quiet ledges beside the sea,
calm blue waters,
mysterious fog-covered waters,
angry wind and wave powered waters.
Find the moon goddess in the milky way
and the searing sun god over desert sand.
Hear the bear hoots on the mountain
and the cicada beside the field.

Longevity, wealth, health, virtue, natural death
have their place:
They are the goal of our every days.
But adventure, get lost, throw off all cares!
Be a sojourner
without place, between, wandering, lost,
abandoned,
in worlds of countless beauties
and eternal wonders.

It is the year of the pig
faithful, ambitious,
intelligent consumer,
a family animal,
domestic, content, successful,
who lives so well
the butcher pays a visit.
For every pig safe in the pen
there is a boar in the forest
dangerous and wild.
Alas, chaos accompanies our civilization:
cold, storm,
tragic events,
dragon energy.

We listen, we seek meanings,
we gather in circles
of our wider kinship.
Around us, warm inside,
the storms of civilization and chaos
whirl for our new beginnings.

DRAGON CHIMES

Sound emanates from the stuff of earth,
vibrations from the deep,
and among creatures of the clouds.

It is living sound,
vibrations from before time,
coursing through before space,
felt in fiber and fabric of knowing.

Every vibration, a clash of elements,
the conflict of surfaces,
the transmission of alarm,
thrills extremities of response.

It is violence and harmony together,
war and peace.
It is the clamor of despair,
the sublime transporting One.

I cannot discern the chaos of cells
that wave and break upon shores
of pure vibration.

I cannot picture the frenzy
of emerging overtones
that leap from one misery
into another more sublime excitation.

Never-ending transformations
continue outward or inward
to other worlds,
to heights or depths
sublime or torn apart,
as frequencies rise or fall.

Dragon chimes
taken into this alien hand,
break into levels unseen,
harmonies and disasters unknown.

We presume to understand
conflicts we witness,
to transform them into harmonies
longed for in story and song.

We presume to know boundaries
of self and society.
But we know only harmonies
this moment sends
to break into tomorrow.

I would like to know, as I long,
that this hand increases harmony
and lessons chaos of conflict,
but I have only the humility of hope
as sound drifts silent
to my ears.

Sound emanates from the stuff of earth,
vibrations from the deep,
and among creatures of the clouds.

ALI, HASAN, HUSAYN

Earth lies quiet:
    the white snow of New England,
    the brown dust of Iran.

Music eternal flows into consciousness:
    notes pour into the well of silence,
    sounds of some far distant sadness
        deep within the world.

The Dervish sings of the prophet's son-in-law, Ali,
    and his two sons, Hasan and Husayn,
    killed by assassins thirteen centuries ago.
    Their tragic endings left a void
        that could not be closed.

To mourn is to care for the land they left.
To mourn is to place life, in all its perplexity,
    into transient time.
To mourn is to bring together neighbor with neighbor
    in a common recognition.

Own your grief
    for it is the grief of life.

Own your grief
        for it honors: father, mother, brother, sister.
Own your grief
        for you mourn your own passing.
Own your grief
        for it connects you in the sadness of the world.

Earth lies quiet.
Music eternal flows into consciousness.
Ali, Hasan, Husayn, rise and rest
        in the reaches of time.

FULL MOON ASCENDING

Full moon ascending
at the equinox,
gently, assuredly,
rising from earth
to meet sky.

Bright mottled orb,
hare with mortar and pestle
mixing herbal elixirs,
auspicious.

Casting upon the snow-formed landscape
a blue illumination,
shadowed trees across
ground portrayed in play of soft shadow.

Nighttime magic upon heart's imagining,
still peace, awaiting the dance of spirits,
awaiting blessings of the Queen Mother,
boons of peace and delight.

Full moon ascending
at the equinox,
gently, assuredly,
rising from earth
to meet sky.

Consider your heart
as the season hinges toward hope.
Imagine new beginnings
Across this gentle night.

Picture the carrion crow
in the oak tree,
the fox in its den,

the sparrow nestled
in the green hedge.

We have only the dance of light
shimmering behind all forms
forshadowing the pink dawn
long after the waxing moon has set.

How strange with blue snow
clinging to every bough
to be speaking of new birth,
buds greening and flowers.

Full moon ascending
at the equinox,
gently, assuredly,
rising from earth
to meet sky.

KUAN YIN: A Story

Grandfather Chu and his grand-daughter, Lia, journeyed from their village on the river to the city to visit a famous art museum. In the first room they saw a large Kuan Yin, tranquil, seated with an arm resting over one knee. The statue had blue and red patches as if it once had been painted. It was so peaceful. Lia couldn't decide whether it was a man or a woman and Grandfather assured her that for this sculpture it didn't matter. Then they saw a large stone Maitreya. It looked to Lia as if it had been rolled out like a scroll, a graceful curved formal pose with a most benevolent face. She stared at that benign smile, looking -- it seemed -- directly at her. She would never forget that smile as if the whole world were smiling for her.

Next Lia stopped at a smaller bronze altar piece. There was a seated Amitabha Buddha, with two Bodhisattvas and seven former Buddhas floating in clouds, two demons and two guardian lions. Lia noticed each piece could be detached from the altar and put back again on their holders. Lia dared not touch for it was a museum. But she imagined how it would be to take them off and decorate them and put them back with little rituals.

Just then Grandfather caught up with her, quickly glanced at the altar and said, "Oh, yes, the Sui Dynasty, a very superstitious time," and with a wave of his hand, as if to dismiss it, began to move to the next piece, a bowl with a fiercely delightful silver dragon wrapped around its rim. Lia hesitated and then followed her grandfather. After all he had lived a long time and he knew so much about old and beautiful things.

Lia had time on their journey home to wonder about superstition and why her Grandfather liked human forms and animals and paintings of mountains. What was wrong with Buddhas flying in clouds and demons peaking out from behind gate posts? Grandfather Chu was a practical man, he liked things to be on solid ground, real things, beautiful forms and proportions. He once pointed out an old pine tree, scarred by lightening, with a crooked trunk, a large gnarled knot on one side. He said, "What a perfect position for a pine so the moon could come to rest in the curve of its trunk."

When spring came it was the custom of the Chu family to walk upstream two villages along the river to visit Grandfather's sister, Ts'ui Ying. The path was beautiful, plum and peach trees blooming, willows yellow. As they neared Great Aunt's home they passed a shrine surrounded by weeping cherry trees. Two young women scurried out from the grove and past them on the path. Just beyond a young man played the lute as blossoms fell around him and onto the flowing river.

Aunt Ts'ui Ying was delighted to see them and plied them with cool delicacies of the Ch'ing Ming festival. There were many stories and Lia was happy to slip away to play with her cousins.

In the late afternoon, Lia saw her Aunt alone walking back along the same path they had come by that morning. She decided to follow her and when Aunt Ts'ui turned into the little shrine Lia followed her. Aunt Ts'ui placed a tiny bowl of rice before the statue and sat quietly while Lia snuggled beside her. The altar before them featured Kuan Yin, goddess of mercy, surrounded by heavenly beings in the clouds, demons peeking from behind gate posts and two guardian lions.

Lia looked up at her Aunt's gentle face; "Very superstitious," Lia said. Ts'ui Ying knew where that had come from. She replied, "Many years ago when I was first married, my baby was still-born. It could not cry. It made no sound. My perfect little daughter had to be buried. I felt so empty I thought I would soon die myself. One morning when I could not sleep I came to this very place at dawn. It was quiet. Pink blossoms and yellow willow branches turned the mist rising from the water below into waves of pink and yellow. Kuan Yin came to me through this mist for she heard my tears. I found hope again in the radiance of that moment. I went on to give birth to two beautiful children and in gratitude we built this shrine. Young women come here and all who sorrow come to this quiet refuge to be with Kuan

Yin. I come here every day." The two of them sat in silence until the light reflected gold on the river.

On the way home Lia told Grandfather Chu the story her Great Aunt had told her. "Do you think she is superstitious?" "No," replied Grandfather Chu; "Your Aunt is a remarkable woman. She has created a beautiful place beside the water. And on a spring day from our village you can see blossoms of peach trees and weeping cherry floating down the river to comfort our sorrows and bring joy again to our hearts. We visit Aunt Ts'ui Ying every spring to share our gratitude for blossoms in river mists and the voices of children." Lia felt a glow of happiness fill her heart as they walked home beside the river.

WORLD ADVENTURE

From the embrace of loving hands
I walked out to explore the world.
From the comforts of home
I left to adventure paths of peace and danger.

I walked across meadows,
past houses and barns,
over rolling fields of waving brown grass
with yellow daisies and tiny wild strawberries,
alongside stone walls and a stately oak tree
with horizontal limbs anchoring the slope.

The picture of barn, field and oak
gave warm assurance

of an ordered and plenteous life,
of harvest and cattle
securely feeding each season in turn.

I entered a forest path
winding deeper through thickets,
brushed against pointed and broken limbs,
found tracks of deer and wolf
in wet leaves at my feet.

Every tree hid shadows of mystery,
every sound spoke of legends
of how I could lose my way,
forget the path for rumors of magic ponds,
be found by thieves or dangerous dragons
hidden in caves behind hemlocks and spruce.

I was climbing now the steep and craggy mountain
and came to cliffs, slippery, steep, rotten.
There were wind swept bushes with thorns
and slippery lichens of red, yellow, green and grey,
a copper snake disappeared into rocks
as I stepped over a fallen cedar.
A mountain lion stood fiercely on a ledge
across a chasm through which roared white water.

At the summit I could sit above the east cliff
and watch the slopes and valleys below,
the same rushing water becoming a stream,
then a winding river to the far off sea.

As it seemed two worlds were meeting:
the giving world of rushing water and rock,
the receiving world forming clouds and rain
for the great return.

Across the summit, from the west cliff,
I could see below, barrens and a desert,
with dunes stretching in the glistening sun,
a great dryness shifting and flowing in the wind.
It received no clouds and gave none.
Only the clear and relentless sun
sparkled and danced in the whirling heat.

Night came upon the summit
and the world became one shape --
to the east and west, north and south --
one sound, one motion in the dark.

Morning found me with family and friends
in my home village.
The chieftain had died in the night
and we sat in a close circle, clasping hands,
through tears speaking of his qualities and adventures.

But now part of me sees an oak tree,
a lion on a cliff,
billions of grains of sand shifting in the sun
and a long winding river flowing to the sea.

NOTES
For Meditations and Photographs

Cover is a sea scene neutral enough to give a place for the title. I have lived near or at the edge of the sea most of my life. The content of poems comes profoundly from the landscape of New England giving grounds for my excursions in our shared planet and kinship in its life.

Flyleaf is a wall painting at Haein-sa Temple in the Mt. Kaya area, South Korea.

Dedication pages have pictures of the buildings of the two congregations for whom most of these meditations were written. The picture of the Unitarian Universalist Congregation in Andover was taken on one of those rare days of the year when the sun reaches the front of the building as it faces slightly west of due north. The worship room of the First Parish Unitarian in Kennebunk contains 6 thousand square feet of trompe l'oeuil painting in a Greek Revival design. I was minister in Kennebunk, 1975-1992 and in Andover, 1992-2002.

FOREWORD is accompanied by photographs of a stairway in Greece and pictograph figures at the Palatki Ruins near Sedona, AZ.

INTRODUCTION is accompanied by a rowboat on Ingraham's Point at the end of our street in Rockland, ME, in bushes with the sea beyond. A second photo is of an Anasazi pectograph in Mesa Verde National Park.

1. p.10. *OUT OF THE VOID*, 1989. I love this particular photograph of the Taj Mahal, taken in the early morning when the tones were still soft. Second photo is of a circle and spiral design on Indian pottery in Mississippi. Note that the spiral is counterclockwise, the direction of spiritual alternatives. Our everyday routines are clockwise.

2. p.13. *TREE: IT IS THERE*, 1996. Picture is an oak tree at Avebury, England.

3. p.15. *SMELL OF SPRING*, 2002. The magnolia tree in the photograph stood in our front lawn on Chestnut Street in Andover.

4. p.17. *BLOSSOMS UPON THE BODY OF EARTH*, 1996. There was a world of life just outside my study window and door there. The weeping cherry blossoms were those referenced in the poem.

5. p.20. *LIFE FORGETS*, 1997, a meditation for Passover. Photo is of a pharaoh, probably Rameses III, in the Karnak Temple in Luxor, Egypt, taken in 1991. Second picture was taken of the ritual tray at one of our Seder celebrations in the Andover congregation.

6. p23. *ONE OF US WALKED IN GALILEE*, 1994. This meditation was for Palm Sunday accompanied with 160 slides of the life of Jesus with stained glass images from Europe and America. Picture is a wall fresco by Fra Angelico located in a monk's room at St. Marc's Monastery in Florence, Italy. Fra Angelico was a member of the order and was buried at St. Marc's.

7. p.25. *LIFE SACRIFICED, LIFE GAINED*, 1994, Easter Sunday. For the Argos reference in this poem see *Archetype of the Spirit*, p. 144. Photograph is of a Celtic crucifix standing in Carnac, France.

8. p.28. *EASTER EGG ENCHANTMENT*, 1998, Easter Sunday. Photograph was the altar arrangement at the Unitaria, Prague, Czech Republic in 1991.

9. p.31. *CROCUS BLOSSOMS*, 2001, Easter Sunday. Crocus blossoms were in Keukenhof Gardens in the Netherlands.

10. p.32. *SPRING BODHISATTVAS*, 1995. This meditation was inspired by chapter 15 in the Lotus Sutra (chapter 14 in the Kern trans. of the India version). Photograph is of the hand of a statue of the Buddha with a pilgrim's flower in its palm. Second picture is of the Colossal Merciful Buddha, Popchusa Temple, South Korea. Another view can be seen in my *Archetype of the Spirit*, p. 117.

11. p.35. *WINGS INDIGO IN THE DAWN*, 1997. The pictures illustrate the story of a journey up the steep trail as a pilgrim to Popchusa Temple in South Korea in 1996. If you look closely at the top of the rock pyramid you will see the indigo wings of the dragonfly.

12. p.37. *108 BEADS*, 2000, Wesak Sunday. Photograph is of Buddhist prayer beads given me by a priest in a worship hall on Mt. Hiei near Kyoto, Japan. Second picture is of a Judas tree in our back yard in Andover.

13. p.40. *BELTANE COMING*, 2001. Picture is the Maypole ceremony referred to in the meditation taken at Westminster Abby in 1991 during a sabbatical leave from the Kennebunk congregation.

14. p.42. *TAPESTRY OF LIFE*, 1998, Beltane Sunday. Blue Heron was photographed in the Spiggot River beside the Andover Organ Co. (old Arlington Mill) in Lawrence, MA.

15. p.44. *A VOICE DIVINE*, 1999. I wrote this poem sitting on the piazza of our home in Rockland, ME, in 1999. I was on a sabbatical and spent a month here to see what it might be as an eventual place to retire. As you can see my response was positive! My mother had just transferred ownership to me, a house built by my great grandparents on land that has been in my family for seven generations. I spent many happy childhood summers here. First photograph is of a late afternoon western sun in the Nile Valley, Egypt, 1991. Second photo is of a tree and house in Cushing, ME overlooking St. George Bay.

16. p.46. *FATAL CRISIS*, 1986. I wrote this as a part of the grief process after the death of my second wife, Mona. If you can write it is important to do so, to commit thoughts to paper giving them closure on the way to new responses in the turmoil of grieving. Photographs are of a seagull and hemlocks with a blurred background of fall leaves.

17. p.48. *FOR MOLLY*, 2001. Meditation was for my Yoga teacher, friend and parishioner, the Sunday after her death. Photograph is of the 5 storied ancient wooden pagoda of the Toji Temple in Kyoto, Japan. Second photo is of the road leading into Kaziranga National Park in India with early morning mists.

18. p.51. *EVE / MY MOTHER'S WORK*, Mother's Day, 1993. Picture is of my mother in 1981, preparing carrots from her garden. Second picture is of a water scene.

19. p.54. *FOR MEMORIAL DAY*, Memorial Day Sunday, 1993. Since this photograph the flag holder has disappeared from my fourth great grandfather's grave in Seaview Cemetery on Jameson's Point, Rockland, ME.

20. p.56. *KNOXVILLE*, 2008. This was given for the Unitarian Universalist Fellowship in Edgecomb, ME, on the Sunday following the shootings there. Photograph is of a statue in Prague, Czech Republic.

21. p. 58. *GRIEF TO GRATITUDE*, 2001. Photograph pictures a bamboo grove at the Huntington Museum Gardens in Pasadena, CA, where my sister, Ann, was chief gardener. Beneath the reflections are the deep and dark waters, symbol of the human unconscious.

22. p.60. *FOURTH OF JULY*, 1989. Fortuitously this photograph was backwards in my slide scanner and I like this compostion better than its reverse. It was taken at the breakwater off Jameson's Point in Rockland Harbor.

23. p.63. *REMEMBERED IN THE FABRIC ONGOING*, 2002. This was the meditation for the last worship gathering I led as minister of the UU Congregation in Andover. I captured this sailing vessel in the fog from the deck of the North Haven Ferry in Rockland Harbor.

24. p.65. *TAKE A CHILD'S HAND*, 1997. Picture is of my grandson, Vann Brazz, following his mother. Mosquito was in Maine, lily pads in Massachusetts.

25. p.68. *SUMMER STORM*, written for the UU Congregation in Ellsworth, ME, July, 2008. As I preached on Charles Darwin, this meditation pictured what in my imagination it must have been for early humans in an electric storm. It is inspired by Jane Goodall's wonderful book on the chimpanzees of Africa. Pictures are of a storm at sea off Sounion, Greece and of granite ledge and water.

26. p.70. *SCRIPTURES*, 1995. Pictured is a wall painting at Haein-sa Temple, South Korea.

27. p.72. *ALLAH*, 2001. Photograph shows the horizon west of the Step Pyramid, the start of a thousand miles of desert. For another picture taken from the same area but facing south see *Archetype of the Spirit*, p. 102.

28. p.74. . *TAKE YOUR TROUBLES TO THE NILE*, 1991. One memory I brought back from a sabbatical was the power of the Nile to ameliorate the harsh dry air and bustle of Cairo in the evening. My sabbatical from the Kennebunk First Parish began in Egypt and ended in England five months later. It was a pilgrimage to numerous sites of our spiritual heritage in 15 countries.

29. p.76. *FOR SARVA DHARMA SAMELANA,* 1993. "Religious people meeting together." This meeting followed on the World Congress of IARF in Bangalore, India. I gave this meditation as part of the Unitarian Universalist worship for this gathering. The backdrop for the stage is all hand woven flowers behind those seated in this photograph.

30. p.78. *EARTH SWALLOWED THEM*, 1993 with 80 slides of everyday life in India. This meditation followed the Maharashtra earthquake. Picture is of an

Indian family in Mysore, India.

31. p.80. *LIFE IS NOT FAIR*, 2000. I suppose the execution of chickens for our food is a rather extreme subject for the accompanying photograph but it is part of our lives. My father wielded the ax while four grandchildren, including my daughters Tamsin and Bradbury, plucked off the feathers.

32. p.82. *FATIMA*, 1997. Photograph is one of four windows above altar of St. Wilfrid's Anglican church in Scrooby, England, illustrating the last words of Jesus; "I was an hungred and ye gave me meat, I was thirsty and ye gave me drink, I was naked and ye clothed me, I was sick and ye visited me."

33. p.84. *WATER*, 1992. About this time of year many congregations hold their ingathering water ceremonies. Pictures include marsh grass and rushing water at the Kennebunk Light and Power dam on the Mousam River.

34. p.86. *STRANGE RESTLESS SIGNS*, 2005. Photograph is of Shiva Nataraja, a bronze I found in Mysore, India.

35. p.88. *HEARTHSIDE HORRORS*, for the Sunday following 9/11. It tells of a nightmare I had the previous night. Photograph is of lower Manhattan from the water in 1991.

36. p.90. *KOL NIDRE*, for the High Holy Days, 1994. Photograph is of our front walk in Andover under the influence of a glorious Japanese maple. Others following are of fall leaves in the Andover area, including the wide Merrimack River.

37. p.95. *AUTUMN MEETING*, 1997. Poem describes many hours with my Great Uncle, Edwin B. Rollins, and imagines a time when I could be in my 90s. He lived to be 102. Birches were in New Hampshire.

38. p.97. *A STRANGE WONDERMENT*, 1998. As the photograph shows, we had to replace the old bird feeder so that the birds could find their share of seeds.

39. p.99. *TO HOLD DEEP SHADOWS CLOSE*, 2000, for Samhain Sunday. Picture is of my younger brother, David, on his last birthday.

40. p.101. *FAR MORE THAN MEETS THE EYE*, 2001. Photo is of my daughters ascending the path from the ocean to the field at my parents' farm in Westport, ME.

41. p.103. *HUNTER'S MOON*, 1997. Deer was photographed near the north rim of the Grand Canyon in AZ.

42. p.105. *WHAT WILL OUR CHILDREN REMEMBER ABOUT US?*, 1992. Pictured is a window of the First Universalist Church in Pittsfield, ME, showing Jesus meeting with the Temple teachers at age 12.

43. p.107. *MOBILIZE FOR WOMEN'S LIVES*, 1989. This was the invocation for the "Sunrise Event" in the national Mobilize for Women's Lives, held at the First Parish Unitarian in Kennebunk, November 12, 1989. It was covered by NBC news and others. The estimated attendance was 2500 filling the meeting house upstairs and down, and the side lawn and street outside. Photographs are of a statue in Germany and a traditional Korean dance performed August 1996. This folk fan dance of the Seolhwa tale, forms a flower blooming in the snow. It was given at the 29th IARF World Congress held at Wonkwang University (headquarters of Won Buddhism), Ikson City, South Korea.

44. p.109. *FOR THE SHARING OF BREAD*, 1996. In Andover we created a tradition of sharing bread at Thanksgiving. The congregation would sit in a circle around a round table of freshly baked bread brought in from homes. With linen napkins, ironed and starched, we would break and share several of the loaves. Picture is of the market at the French village of Divonne les Bains.

45. p.110. *NOVEMBER HARVEST*, 1993. Picture is of a spruce forest scene in Fundy Provincial Park in New Brunswick. Preceding the meditation are pictures of the First Church In Plymouth, MA, Unitarian Universalist, founded in 1620, and a stained glass window behind the pulpit depicting the signing of the Mayflower Compact. I am descended from one shown, Richard Warren.

46. p.112. *THANKSGIVING*, Thanksgiving Sunday 1987. Photograph is of our family Thanksgiving Dinner in 1973. Note the winter menu with the absence of fresh green vegetables. The fruit décor at the center of the table of course is an aberration. Pictured are my great aunt and uncle, Professor Edwin and Mabel (Kalloch) Rollins, aunt, Dorothy Pearson, usual host of our Thanksgivings, my mother, Eleanor, my daughter, Tamsin, and father, Elford. Not shown were daughter, Bradbury, and first wife, Caroline.

47. p.114. *AS A LAKSHMI LAMP*, 2001. Photograph is of a small South Indian lamp I bought in 1993 in Bangalore, India. It is bronze, about 175 years old, from the village of Thanjawar in Tamil Nadu. The family had five daughters and needed money for dowry. I hope my stewardship does justice to the piety of generations of this family. Facing is a pilgrim at the Janmastumi Festival at the MahaLakshmi Temple in Mumbai, India, taking her offering to the surf below the temple.

48. p.116. *MACCABEUS*, for Hanukkah, 1987. Photograph is a window at the Fifth Avenue Reformed Temple, Pittsburgh, PA. Hebrew reads, "Come into His gates with thankfulness."

49. p119. *A DARK TIME*, 1993. Photograph is in the evening over Portsmouth, NH. The second photograph is of snow and sea in late afternoon, Kennebunk Beach, ME.

50. p.121. *GOLDEN SEED*, Christmas Eve, 1997. Photograph is part of a Marc Chagall window in the Fraumunster Church, Zurich, Switzerland.

51. p.123. *BLINKING LIGHTS ON A BARE TREE*, Christmas Sunday 1996. Photograph is of an antique electric ornament given to me by my great uncle, Edwin B. Rollins.

52. p.124. *MIDNIGHT MASS*, Christmas Eve. Photograph is of the black Madonna in Notre Dame Cathedral in Chartres, France.

53. p.127. *WINTER APPLE TREE*, Christmas, 1986. The tree photographed was in our back yard in Andover. The tree described in the meditation was next to the Maine Turnpike in Wells, ME. Second picture is of ice and salt marsh weeds at Kennebunk Beach.

54. p.129. *IN THE PAUSING TIME*, New Year, 1995. Photographs are of an old white pine, all that remains in a desolate gravel pit buried in new fallen snow, Weymouth, MA, and a snowdrift at Kennebunk Beach.

55. p.130. *DREAMS / RESOLUTIONS*, New Year, 1998. Abstract night scene was photographed in Fort Worth, Texas, during a General Assembly. Snow scene was in Weymouth, MA.

56. p.133. *TO BUILD AND TO BUILD AGAIN*, 1994. Icicles were on a Maine pine.

57. p.134. *WHERE IS GOD ?*, 1998. Photographs are of a human skeleton at Indian mounds in south central, Ohio and an electric transmission pole in Portsmouth, NH.

58. p.136. *JESUS COULD NOT HAVE WALKED*, 1997. Photograph is of a scene in modern day Prague, Czech Republic. I like the juxtaposition of a first century event with the electric wires of twentieth century life.

59. p.138. *PRUNING THE APPLE TREE*, 1998. Picture is our apple tree in Andover after an ice storm.

60. p.140. *YEAR 4693*, Chinese New Year, 1995. This meditation explores both the Confucian and the Taoist values in this holiday. Picture is of a Confucian scholar, perhaps Confucius himself, Confucian Temple, Beijing, China.

61. p.143. *DRAGON CHIMES*, 1994. Pictures are of a pair of dragon chimes and details on Taoist and Buddhist Incense burners in Beijing.

62. p.146. *ALI, HASAN, HUSAYN*, 1993. Photograph is of the ancient Ahmed Ibn-Tulun Mosque, Cairo, 1991.

63. p.147. *FULL MOON ASCENDING*, at the equinox, 2000. Photograph is of drifting sand and snow on Kennebunk Beach.

64. p148. *KUAN YIN: A STORY*, 2001. Photographs are an abstract sculpture of mother and child, St. Paul's Cathedral, London, England and a Kuan Yin in my Rockland study.

65. p151. *WORLD ADVENTURE*, 1991. Photographs are of a mountainside visual pun, Yosemite National Park, CA and of a wonderful little canyon through limestone in Shelburne Falls, MA.

NOTES. P.154. *SHIVA AND PARVATI*, a sulpture among thousands, on Hoipaleswara Temple, Halebid, India.

ALSO AVAILABLE FROM RED BARN PUBLISHING

SPIRITUALITY AND PSYCHOLOGY by Peter Tufts Richardson

ARCHETYPE OF THE SPIRIT. Rescued from the rarified and esoteric on the one hand and the trance of everyday on the other, Archetype of the Spirit documents a presence in our lives very near to us and of remotely ancient tradition. Employing images and motifs found universally in local traditions world around, this book correlates these with psychological type, the MBTI,™ Jung's compass and the Four Spiritualities of our humanity. [quality paperback, 172 pgs, 108 illustrations, bibliography, index, 2007, $24.95]

FOUR SPIRITUALITIES. Explores and describes four parallel spiritual paths found in every branch of human religion: the Journey of Unity, the Journey of Devotion, the Journey of Works and the Journey of Harmony. They are correlated with the MBTI.™ In this way an individual can examine how their unique personality resonates with the most compatible way forward. [quality paperback, 245 pgs, 10 illustrations, bibliography, index, 1996, $18.95.]

GROWING YOUR SPIRITUALITY. This workshop leader guide accompanies Four Spiritualities and Archetype of the Spirit. Included are introductions, exercises and background readings. A special section provides for interfaith relationships. [typescript, spiral bound, 2001, $12.00]

UNITARIAN UNIVERSALIST HISTORY by Peter Tufts Richardson

THE BOSTON RELIGION. Is a window into the entire history and significance of American Unitarianism. In tracing the unique qualities of the 74 Unitarian churches that have been organized within the Boston city limits you will find most of the movement's leaders, all the major theological currents and controversies and the impact of the religion on American culture and development. [hardcover, sewn, dust jacket, 256 pgs, 139 illustrations, bibliography, index, $29.95]

ALSO AVAILABLE continued

EXPLORING UNITARIAN UNIVERSALIST IDENTITY. The author's Minns Lectures for 2005. Four key issues are elaborated, most particularly "From Unsectarian Sect To Multifaith Faith." [quality paperack, 121 pgs, 16 illustrations, expanded notes, bibliography, index, $14.95]

LOCAL HISTORY by Eleanor Motley Richardson

MECHANIC STREET: Uncovering the History of a Maine Neighborhood
While this is the story of one ordinary street in Rockland, Maine, it could be the story of any street, your street. This book gives you the tools to research your own neighborhood and a fascinating read too. 162 pages, profusely illustrated, indexed. Hardbound: $29.95. Softbound: $18.95.

NORTH HAVEN SUMMERS: An Oral History
"Of course that last summer she came in an ambulance. She wasn't the first grandmother to do it when she could no longer get to North Haven under her own steam." So begins the story of the summer community on a lovely island in Penobscot Bay, ME. This book describes the drama, humor and adventure of life on this small island told by more than 90 summer and year-round residents. 258 pages, 167 photos, indexed. Hardbound only: $29.95.

TO ORDER or for INFORMATION: Contact the authors at ptemr@aol.com or 22 Mechanic St., Rockland, ME, 04841. Please visit our web site:

WWW.REDBARNROCKLAND.COM